HOUGHTON MIFFLIN

Georgia Science

HOUGHTON MIFFLIN   BOSTON

Program Authors

William Badders
Director of the Cleveland Mathematics and Science Partnership
Cleveland Municipal School District, Cleveland, Ohio

Douglas Carnine, Ph.D.
Professor of Education
University of Oregon, Eugene, Oregon

Bobby Jeanpierre, Ph.D.
Assistant Professor, Science Education
University of Central Florida, Orlando, Florida

James Feliciani
Supervisor of Instructional Media and Technology
Land O' Lakes, Florida

Carolyn Sumners, Ph.D.
Director of Astronomy and Physical Sciences
Houston Museum of Natural Science, Houston, Texas

Catherine Valentino
Author-in-Residence
Houghton Mifflin, West Kingston, Rhode Island

Content Consultants
See Teacher's Edition for a complete list.

Printed in the U.S.A.

ISBN 13: 978-0-618-88489-6
ISBN 10: 0-618-88489-0

2 3 4 5 6 7 8 9-VH-16 15 14 13 12 11 10 09 08

Georgia Teacher Reviewers

Peggy Baugh
Douglas County Board of Education
Douglasville, Georgia

Douglas O. Carroll
White Bluff Elementary
Savannah, Georgia

Vanessa Hooks Denison
Garden City Elementary
Garden City, Georgia

Theresa Drago
Collins Elementary School
Augusta, Georgia

Kimberly Geralds
Settles Bridge Elementary
Suwanee, Georgia

Amy R. Hillman
Freedom Park Elementary
Augusta, Georgia

Lisa Iennaccaro-Hills
Chattahoochee Elementary
Cumming, Georgia

Megan Horsley
Sawnee Primary School
Cumming, Georgia

Marsha Mattson
Bascomb Elementary
Woodstock, Georgia

Janyce Moreland
Emma Hutchinson Elementary
Atlanta, Georgia

Roxanne Peterson
Pine Street Elementary
Conyers, Georgia

Barbara Ramps
Liberty Elementary
Midway, Georgia

James Roszkowiak
Spencer Elementary
Savannah, Georgia

Donna Smith
Russell Elementary
Smyrna, Georgia

Debbie Wallace
Sawnee Primary School
Cumming, Georgia

Contents

UNIT A
Earth Science

Big Idea Changes in the sky can be observed throughout the year.

Reading in Science: Start with a Poem 2

Science in Georgia 4

Hands-On Project:

    How Can School Grounds Change? 8

Chapter 1

Weather Patterns 10

Vocabulary Preview 12

S2E3a   **Lesson 1** How Does Weather Change? 14

S2E3a   Extreme Science: Take Cover! 22

S2E2c   **Lesson 2** What Is the Pattern of the Seasons? 24

S2E2c   Focus On: Health and Safety:

    Staying Safe in the Sun 30

S2L1b   **Lesson 3** How Do Living Things Change

    with the Seasons? 32

S2CS6d   **Careers in Science** .39

S2CS2a   **Links for Home and School** 40

S2E2D   **Performance Task** .41

    Review and CRCT Prep 42

Chapter 2   **Motions in the Sky** **44**

Vocabulary Preview **46**

S2E1a   **Lesson 1**   What Makes Up the Solar System?. **48**

S2E1a   Extreme Science: Orion's Surprise **54**

S2E2b   **Lesson 2**   How Does Earth Move?. **56**

S2E2b   Focus On: Readers' Theater:
         A Shadow Fable **62**

S2E2d   **Lesson 3**   How Does the Moon Move?. **66**

S2CS5a   Focus On: Literature:
         The Tale of Rabbit and Coyote **72**

S2E1a   **Lesson 4**   What Stars Can You See? **74**

S2CS6d   **People in Science** **81**

S2E2d   **Links for Home and School** **82**

S2E2B   **Performance Task** **83**

Review and CRCT Prep **84**

CRCT Prep **86**

S2E1a   **Unit Wrap-Up** **88**

Chattahoochee National Forest, Georgia

v

Contents

UNIT B
Physical Science

Big Idea The motion of objects can be observed and measured.

Reading in Science: Start with a Poem......90

Science in Georgia 92

Hands-On Project: Math Relay Game 96

Chapter 3

Comparing Matter 98

Vocabulary Preview 100

S2P1a   **Lesson 1** How Can You Compare Matter?...........102

S2P1b   **Extreme Science:** Sand to Glass 110

S2P1b   **Lesson 2** How Does Matter Change?................112

S2P1a   **Focus On: Technology:**

     Changing Matter to Make Coins 120

S2P1   **Lesson 3** How Does Matter Look Up Close?..........122

S2CS6d   **Careers in Science** 127

S2CS2d   **Links for Home and School** 128

S2P1A   **Performance Task** 129

   Review and CRCT Prep 130

Chapter 4

Objects in Motion 132
Vocabulary Preview 134

S2P3a **Lesson 1** How Do Things Move? 136

S2P3b Extreme Science: Fast, Faster, Fastest! 142

S2P3a **Lesson 2** What Do Forces Do? 144

S2P3a Focus On: Readers' Theater:
Safety in Motion 150

S2P3b **Lesson 3** What Can You Do with Motion? 154

S2CS6d **Careers in Science** 161

S2CS2c **Links for Home and School** 162

S2P2A **Performance Task** 163

Review and CRCT Prep 164

Chapter 5

Heat and Light 166
Vocabulary Preview 168

S2P2a **Lesson 1** What Is Heat?. 170

S2P2b Focus On: History of Science:
The Warming Sun 176

S2P2b **Lesson 2** What Is Light? 178

S2P2a Extreme Science: Light Trap 184

S2CS2a **Links for Home and School** 186

S2P2C **Performance Task** 187

Review and CRCT Prep 188

CRCT Prep 190

Unit Wrap-Up 192

Contents

UNIT C
Life Science

Big Idea Plants and animals meet their needs in different ways.

Reading in Science: Start with a Poem 194

Science in Georgia 196

Hands-On Project:

How Does a Tree Change? 200

Chapter 6   **Plant Life Cycles** 202

Vocabulary Preview 204

S2L1c   **Lesson 1**   How Do Plants Change During

Their Life Cycles? 206

S2L1d   **Extreme Science:** Marvelous Mushrooms 214

S2L1c   **Lesson 2**   What Kind of a Plant Grows from a Seed? . . . 216

S2L1c   **Lesson 3**   How Do Plants of the Same Kind Differ? 222

S2L1c   **Focus On: Technology:** Great Grapes 228

S2L1c   **Lesson 4**   How Do Plants React to Their

Environments? 230

S2CS2a   **Links for Home and School** 236

S2L1c   **Performance Task** 237

S2CS6d   **Careers in Science** 238

S2CS6d   **People in Science** 239

Review and CRCT Prep 240

Chapter 7   **Animal Life Cycles** 242
                  Vocabulary Preview 244

S2L1a   **Lesson 1** Which Baby Animals Look
                      Like Their Parents? 246

S2L1a   **Lesson 2** Which Baby Animals Look
                      Unlike Their Parents? 252

S2CS5a   Extreme Science: Check Out
                    These Chickens 258

S2L1a   **Lesson 3** Where Do Animals Get Their Traits? 260

S2CS5a   Focus On: Technology: Spin a Yarn 266

S2L1a   **Lesson 4** How Do Animals of the Same Kind Differ? . . . 268

S2CS2b   **Links for Home and School** 274

S2L1B   **Performance Task** 275

S2CS6d   **Careers in Science** 276

S2CS6d   **People in Science** 277

                    Review and CRCT Prep 278

                    CRCT Prep 280

S2CS4d   **Unit Wrap-Up** 282

Inquiry Focus Activities

. . . stimulates children's critical thinking and research skills. Children will take opportunities presented to ask questions they are pondering and seek to create new meaning from their experiences with the activities listed here.

EARTH **UNIT A** **SCIENCE**

Directed Inquiry

Compare Weather 15
Measure Heat. 25
Compare Fabrics. 33
Light and Heat 49
Observe Shadows. 57
Moon Phases 67
Star Pictures 75

Use the Sun's Light to
    Change Paper. 50
Change Shadows by Using
    a Flashlight. 59
Show Phases of the Moon. . . . 69
Make a Constellation. 76

Express Lab

See the Wind Move 19
Compare the Weather. 27
Show Changes 34

Performance Tasks

When do the number of
    daylight hours change?. . . . 41
How does your shadow
    change? 83

PHYSICAL **B** SCIENCE

Directed Inquiry

Measure Matter 103
Compare Matter 113
Observe Objects 123
Observe Motion 137
Make Things Move 145
Measure Motion 155
Warm and Cool Places 171
Seeing Things 179

Describe an Object's
    Location 140
Observe a Ball's Motion 147
Measure Motion 157
Make Heat 173
Use Light to Communicate . . 180

Express Lab

Classify Properties 105
Time a Change of State 115
Observe Details 124

Performance Tasks

How are mixtures
    different? 129
How do objects move
    differently? 163
Energy Collage 187

LIFE **C** SCIENCE

Directed Inquiry

Fruits and Seeds 207
Plant Seeds 217
Compare Pea Pods 223
Sprouting Seeds 231
Compare Life Cycles 247
Triops Stages 253
Train Goldfish 261
Measure Handspans 269

Compare Leaf Size 225
Compare Temperature 233
Match Animals 249
Measure How a Frog
    Changes 255
Observe a Learned Behavior . 263
Compare Two Individuals . . . 271

Express Lab

Order a Plant Life Cycle 209
Compare Young Plants to
    Their Parents 219

Performance Tasks

How do growing plants
    change? 237
How do animals change
    as they grow? 275

Using Your Book

The Nature of Science

In the front of your book you will learn about how people explore science.

Every unit in your book has two or more chapters.

The Nature of Science

You Can Do What Scientists Do S10
You Can Think Like a Scientist . . S12
You Can Be an Inventor S18
You Can Make Decisions S22
Science Safety S24

Big Idea! tells you the science idea that connects the content of each lesson.

Independent Books You can read these on your own.

UNIT C

Life Science

Reading in Science 194
Science in Georgia:
Life Science Preview 196
Chapter 6
Plant Life Cycles 202
Chapter 7
Animal Life Cycles 242

Independent Reading

Marvelous Mammals

Are They Look-Alikes?

The Life of a Bean

Big Idea!

Life Science
Plants and animals have life cycles that you can predict.

Fun Facts

Cougars have powerful hind legs. They can spring foward 30 feet in one leap.

193

Every unit begins with a special **Science in Georgia** feature.

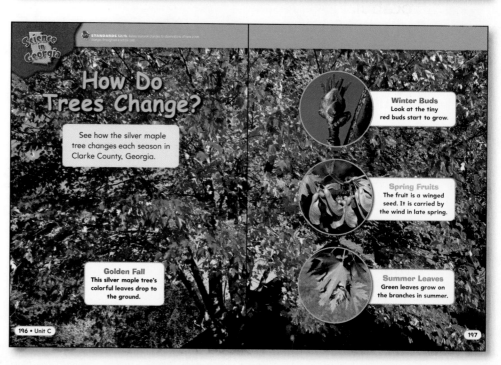

Science in Georgia

STANDARDS S2L1b. Relate seasonal changes to observations of how a tree changes throughout a school year.

How Do Trees Change?

See how the silver maple tree changes each season in Clarke County, Georgia.

Winter Buds
Look at the tiny red buds start to grow.

Spring Fruits
The fruit is a winged seed. It is carried by the wind in late spring.

Golden Fall
This silver maple tree's colorful leaves drop to the ground.

Summer Leaves
Green leaves grow on the branches in summer.

Lesson Preview
gives information
and asks questions
about each lesson.

Chapter **7**

Animal Life Cycles

242

Lesson Preview

LESSON 1 These chicks look alike. How are they like their parents?

LESSON 2 A caterpillar changes as it grows. How does it change?

LESSON 3 This dog can fetch. Why can some dogs do tricks?

LESSON 4 These hamsters are alike in many ways. How are they different?

243

Vocabulary Preview

Introduces important science terms with pictures
and vocabulary skills.

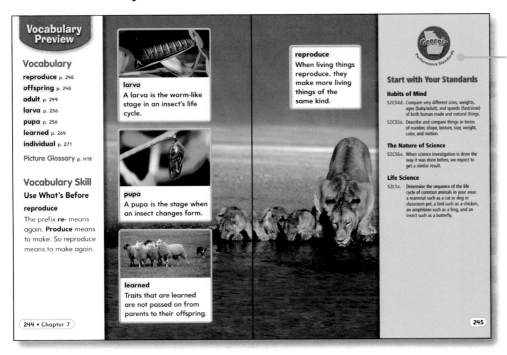

Vocabulary Preview

Vocabulary
reproduce p. 248
offspring p. 248
adult p. 249
larva p. 256
pupa p. 256
learned p. 264
individual p. 271

Picture Glossary p. H18

Vocabulary Skill
Use What's Before
reproduce

The prefix **re-** means
again. **Produce** means
to make. So reproduce
means to make again.

larva
A larva is the worm-like
stage in an insect's life
cycle.

pupa
A pupa is the stage when
an insect changes form.

learned
Traits that are learned
are not passed on from
parents to their offspring.

reproduce
When living things
reproduce, they
make more living
things of the
same kind.

Start with Your Standards

Habits of Mind
S2CS4d. Compare very different sizes, weights,
ages (baby/adult), and speeds (fast/slow)
of both human made and natural things.
S2CS5a. Describe and compare things in terms
of number, shape, texture, size, weight,
color, and motion.

The Nature of Science
S2CS6a. When science investigation is done the
way it was done before, we expect to
get a similar result.

Life Science
S2L1a. Determine the sequence of the life
cycle of common animals in your area:
a mammal such as a cat or dog or
classroom pet, a bird such as a chicken,
an amphibian such as a frog, and an
insect such as a butterfly.

Georgia Science
Performance
Standards are
identified for
each chapter.

244 • Chapter 7

245

Every lesson in your book has two parts.

Part 1: Directed Inquiry

Science and You helps you think about the science facts.

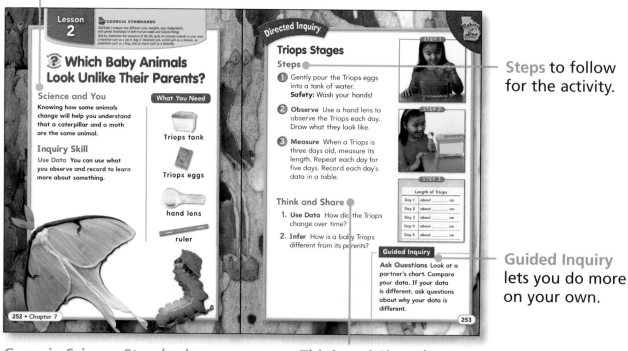

Steps to follow for the activity.

Guided Inquiry lets you do more on your own.

Georgia Science Standards appear throughout the lesson.

Think and Share lets you check what you have learned.

Part 2: Learn by Reading

Vocabulary lists the new science words you will learn. In the text, dark words with yellow around them are new words.

Lesson Wrap-Up

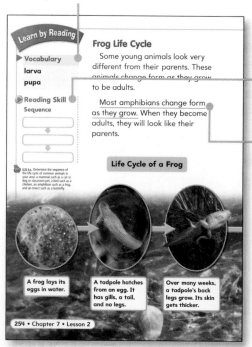

Reading Skill helps you understand the text.

Main Idea is underlined to show you what is important.

After you read, check what you have learned.

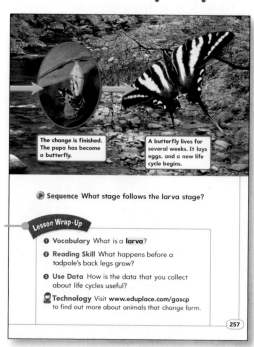

Focus On

Focus On lets you learn more about an important topic. Look for History of Science, Technology, Literature, Readers' Theater—and more.

Extreme Science

Extreme Science compares and contrasts interesting science informaion.

Links and Performance Task

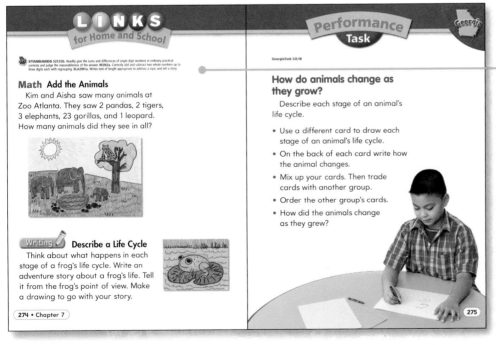

Links connects science to other subject areas.

Performance Task is a chance to show what you know.

You can do these at school or at home.

Review and Unit Practice

These reviews help you to know you are on track with learning Georgia science standards.

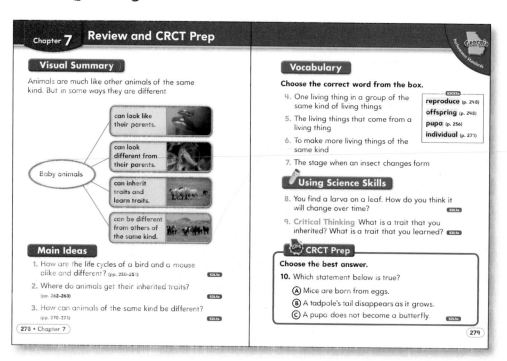

Chapter **7** Review and CRCT Prep

Visual Summary

Animals are much like other animals of the same kind. But in some ways they are different.

Baby animals
- can look like their parents.
- can look different from their parents.
- can inherit traits and learn traits.
- can be different from others of the same kind.

Main Ideas

1. How are the life cycles of a bird and a mouse alike and different? (pp. 250–251)

2. Where do animals get their inherited traits? (pp. 262–263)

3. How can animals of the same kind be different? (pp. 270–271)

278 • Chapter 7

Vocabulary

Choose the correct word from the box.

4. One living thing in a group of the same kind of living things

5. The living things that come from a living thing

6. To make more living things of the same kind

7. The stage when an insect changes form

reproduce (p. 248)
offspring (p. 248)
pupa (p. 256)
individual (p. 271)

Using Science Skills

8. You find a larva on a leaf. How do you think it will change over time?

9. **Critical Thinking** What is a trait that you inherited? What is a trait that you learned?

CRCT Prep

Choose the best answer.

10. Which statement below is true?

   Ⓐ Mice are born from eggs.

   Ⓑ A tadpole's tail disappears as it grows.

   Ⓒ A pupa does not become a butterfly.

279

Unit Wrap-Up

C Wrap-Up

You Can...

STANDARDS S2CS6E

Discover More

How do mother sea lions find their pups?

To find their pups, mother sea lions make a loud trumpet sound. Each mother's sound is different. When the pup hears the sound, it makes a bleating sound back. Mother and pup continue until they find each other. The mother knows for sure which pup is hers by its smell.

Go to **www.eduplace.com/gascp** to learn how animals find their babies.

282 • Unit C

Learn more about science using the **Discover More!** question.

References

Index

Picture Glossary

Health and Fitness Handbook

Science and Math Toolbox

Science and Math Toolbox

Using a Hand Lens H2
Using a Thermometer H3
Using a Ruler H4
Using a Calculator H5
Using a Balance H6
Making a Chart H7
Making a Tally Chart H8
Making a Bar Graph H9

The back of your book includes sections you will refer to again and again.

Start With Your Standards

Characteristics of Science

> Habits of Mind S1

> Nature of Science S3

Content Standards

> Earth Science S4

> Physical Science. S5

> Life Science S6

Characteristics of Science

Habits of Mind

S2CS1 Students will be aware of the importance of curiosity, honesty, openness, and skepticism in science and will exhibit these traits in their own efforts to understand how the world works.

a. Raise questions about the world around them and be willing to seek answers to some of the questions by making careful observations and measurements and trying to figure things out.

S2CS2 Students will have the computation and estimation skills necessary for analyzing data and following scientific explanations.

a. Use whole numbers in ordering, counting, identifying, measuring, and describing things and experiences.

b. Readily give the sums and differences of single-digit numbers in ordinary, practical contexts and judge the reasonableness of the answer.

c. Give rough estimates of numerical answers to problems before doing them formally.

d. Make quantitative estimates of familiar lengths, weights, and time intervals, and check them by measuring.

S2CS3 Students will use tools and instruments for observing, measuring, and manipulating objects in scientific activities.

a. Use ordinary hand tools and instruments to construct, measure, and look at objects.

b. Assemble, describe, take apart, and reassemble constructions using interlocking blocks, erector sets, and other things.

c. Make something that can actually be used to perform a task, using paper, cardboard, wood, plastic, metal, or existing objects.

S2CS4 Students will use the ideas of system, model, change, and scale in exploring scientific and technological matters.

a. Identify the parts of things, such as toys or tools, and identify what things can do when put together that they could not do otherwise.

b. Use a model—such as a toy or a picture—to describe a feature of the primary thing.

c. Describe changes in the size, weight, color, or movement of things, and note which of their other qualities remain the same during a specific change.

d. Compare very different sizes, weights, ages (baby/adult), and speeds (fast/slow) of both human made and natural things.

S2CS5 Students will communicate scientific ideas and activities clearly.

a. Describe and compare things in terms of number, shape, texture, size, weight, color, and motion.

b. Draw pictures (grade level appropriate) that correctly portray features of the thing being described.

c. Use simple pictographs and bar graphs to communicate data.

The Nature of Science

S2CS6 Students will be familiar with the character of scientific knowledge and how it is achieved.

Students will recognize that:

a. When a science investigation is done the way it was done before, we expect to get a similar result.

b. Science involves collecting data and testing hypotheses.

c. Scientists often repeat experiments multiple times and subject their ideas to criticism by other scientists who may disagree with them and do further tests.

d. All different kinds of people can be and are scientists.

S2CS7 Students will understand important features of the process of scientific inquiry.

Students will apply the following to inquiry learning practices:

a. Scientists use a common language with precise definitions of terms to make it easier to communicate their observations to each other.

b. In doing science, it is often helpful to work as a team. All team members should reach their own individual conclusions and share their understandings with other members of the team in order to develop a consensus.

c. Tools such as thermometers, rulers, and balances often give more information about things than can be obtained by just observing things without help.

d. Much can be learned about plants and animals by observing them closely, but care must be taken to know the needs of living things and how to provide for them. Advantage can be taken of classroom pets.

Coverage of these standards occurs in Directed Inquiry, Guided Inquiry, and in other features.

Content Standards

Earth Science

S2E1 Students will understand that stars have different sizes, brightness, and patterns.

a. Describe the physical attributes of stars—size, brightness, and patterns.

Chapter 2: Motions in the Sky

S2E2 Students will investigate the position of sun and moon to show patterns throughout the year.

a. Investigate the position of the sun in relation to a fixed object on earth at various times of the day.

b. Determine how the shadows change through the day by making a shadow stick or using a sundial.

c. Relate the length of the day and night to the change in seasons (for example: Days are longer than the night in the summer.).

d. Use observations and charts to record the shape of the moon for a period of time.

Chapter 1: Weather Patterns
Chapter 2: Motions in the Sky

S2E3 Students will observe and record changes in their surroundings and infer the causes of the changes.

a. Recognize effects that occur in a specific area caused by weather, plants, animals, and/or people.

Chapter 1: Weather Patterns

Physical Science

S2P1 Students will investigate the properties of matter and changes that occur in objects.

a. Identify the three common states of matter as solid, liquid, or gas.

b. Investigate changes in objects by tearing, dissolving, melting, squeezing, etc.

Chapter 3: Comparing Matter

S2P2 Students will identify sources of energy and how the energy is used.

a. Identify sources of light energy, heat energy, and energy of motion.

b. Describe how light, heat, and motion energy are used.

Chapter 5: Heat and Light

S2P3 Students will demonstrate changes in speed and direction using pushes and pulls.

a. Demonstrate how pushing and pulling an object affects the motion of the object.

b. Demonstrate the effects of changes of speed on an object.

Chapter 4: Objects in Motion

Life Science

S2L1 Students will investigate the life cycles of different living organisms.

a. Determine the sequence of the life cycle of common animals in your area: a mammal such as a cat or dog or classroom pet, a bird such as a chicken, an amphibian such as a frog, and an insect such as a butterfly.

b. Relate seasonal changes to observations of how a tree changes throughout a school year.

c. Investigate the life cycle of a plant by growing a plant from a seed and by recording changes over a period of time.

d. Identify fungi (mushrooms) as living organisms.

Chapter 1: Weather Patterns
Chapter 6: Plant Life Cycles
Chapter 7: Animal Life Cycles

The Nature of Science

Science is an adventure. People all over the world do science. You can do science, too. You probably already do.

Start With Your Standards

The Nature of Science

S2CS6 Students will be familiar with the character of scientific knowledge and how it is achieved.

Students will recognize that:

   a. When a science investigation is done the way it was done before, we expect to get a similar result.

   b. Science involves collecting data and testing hypotheses.

   c. Scientists often repeat experiments multiple times and subject their ideas to criticism by other scientists who may disagree with them and do further tests.

   d. All different kinds of people can be and are scientists.

S2CS7 Students will understand important features of the process of scientific inquiry.

Students will apply the following to inquiry learning practices:

   a. Scientists use a common language with precise definitions of terms to make it easier to communicate their observations to each other.

   b. In doing science, it is often helpful to work as a team. All team members should reach their own individual conclusions and share their understandings with other members of the team in order to develop a consensus.

   c. Tools such as thermometers, rulers, and balances often give more information about things than can be obtained by just observing things without help.

   d. Much can be learned about plants and animals by observing them closely, but care must be taken to know the needs of living things and how to provide for them. Advantage can be taken of classroom pets.

The Nature of Science

You Can Do What Scientists Do S10

You Can Think Like a Scientist . . S12

You Can Be an Inventor S18

You Can Make Decisions S22

Science Safety S24

Do What Scientists Do

Meet Fernando Caldeiro, the astronaut. His friends call him Frank. He is training to go into space. When he is not training, he tests computer programs used to run the space shuttle. Before Mr. Caldeiro became an astronaut, he tested new jets. He also worked on space shuttle rockets.

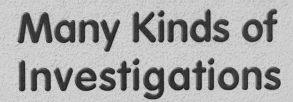
Frank Caldeiro is floating in a jet that gives the feeling of low gravity. This jet is one tool scientists use to learn more about space.
The jet's nickname is the "vomit comet." Can you guess why?

Many Kinds of Investigations

Astronauts carry out many investigations in space. Sometimes they observe Earth and take photos. Other times they do experiments. They may test how plants or animals react to low gravity. They share what they find out with other scientists.

Astronauts learn to fly the space shuttle in machines called simulators. They also learn to use space shuttle tools to collect information.

Think Like a Scientist

Everyone can do science.
To think like a scientist you have to:

▶ ask a lot of questions.

▶ find answers by investigating.

▶ work on a team.

▶ compare your ideas
to those of others.

**What is this lizard
doing? Is it sleeping?
Is it waiting for insects
to fly by? Or, is it doing
something else?**

Use Critical Thinking

When you know the difference between what you observe and what you think about your observation, you are a critical thinker. A fact is an observation that can be checked to make sure it is true. An opinion is what you think about the facts. When you ask someone, "How do you know that?" you are asking for facts.

The lizard lies under the heat lamp for a while. Then it gets food. **I wonder if it must warm up before it can move around?**

I read that a lizard's body temperature falls when the air cools. It warms itself by lying in the sun.

Science Inquiry

You can use **scientific inquiry** to find answers to your questions about the world around you. Say you have seen crickets in the yard.

Observe It seems like crickets chirp very fast on some nights, but slowly on other nights.

Ask a question I wonder, does the speed of cricket chirping change with temperature?

Form an idea I think crickets chirp faster when it's warmer.

Experiment I will need a timer and a thermometer. I will count how many times a cricket chirps in 2 minutes. I will do this when the air temperature is warmer and when the air temperature is cooler.

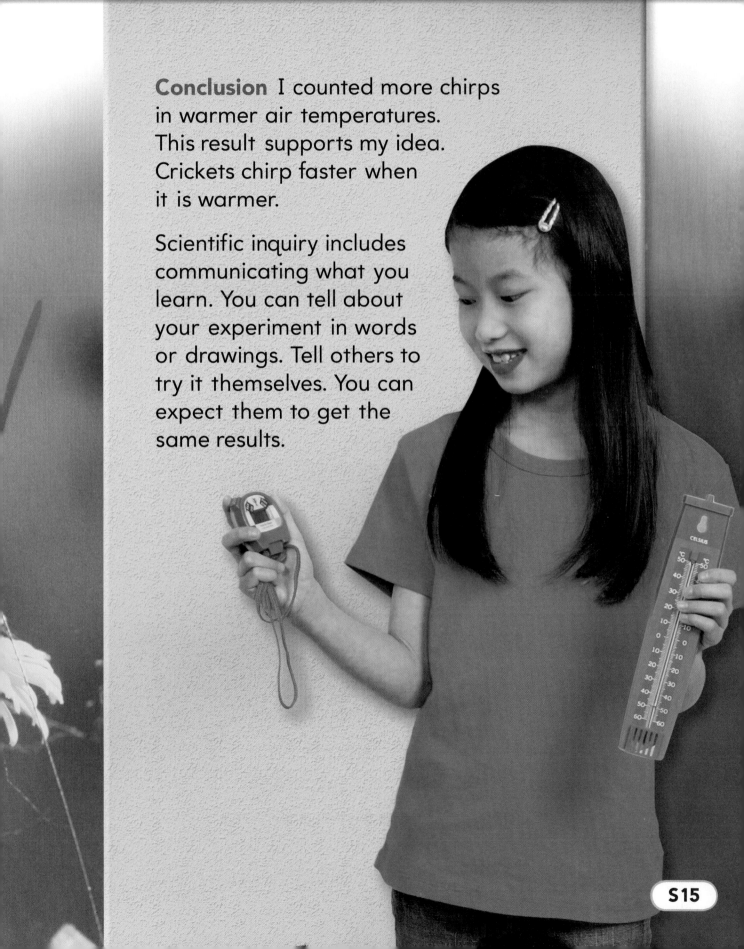

Conclusion I counted more chirps in warmer air temperatures. This result supports my idea. Crickets chirp faster when it is warmer.

Scientific inquiry includes communicating what you learn. You can tell about your experiment in words or drawings. Tell others to try it themselves. You can expect them to get the same results.

S15

Inquiry Process

Here is a process that some scientists follow to answer questions and make new discoveries.

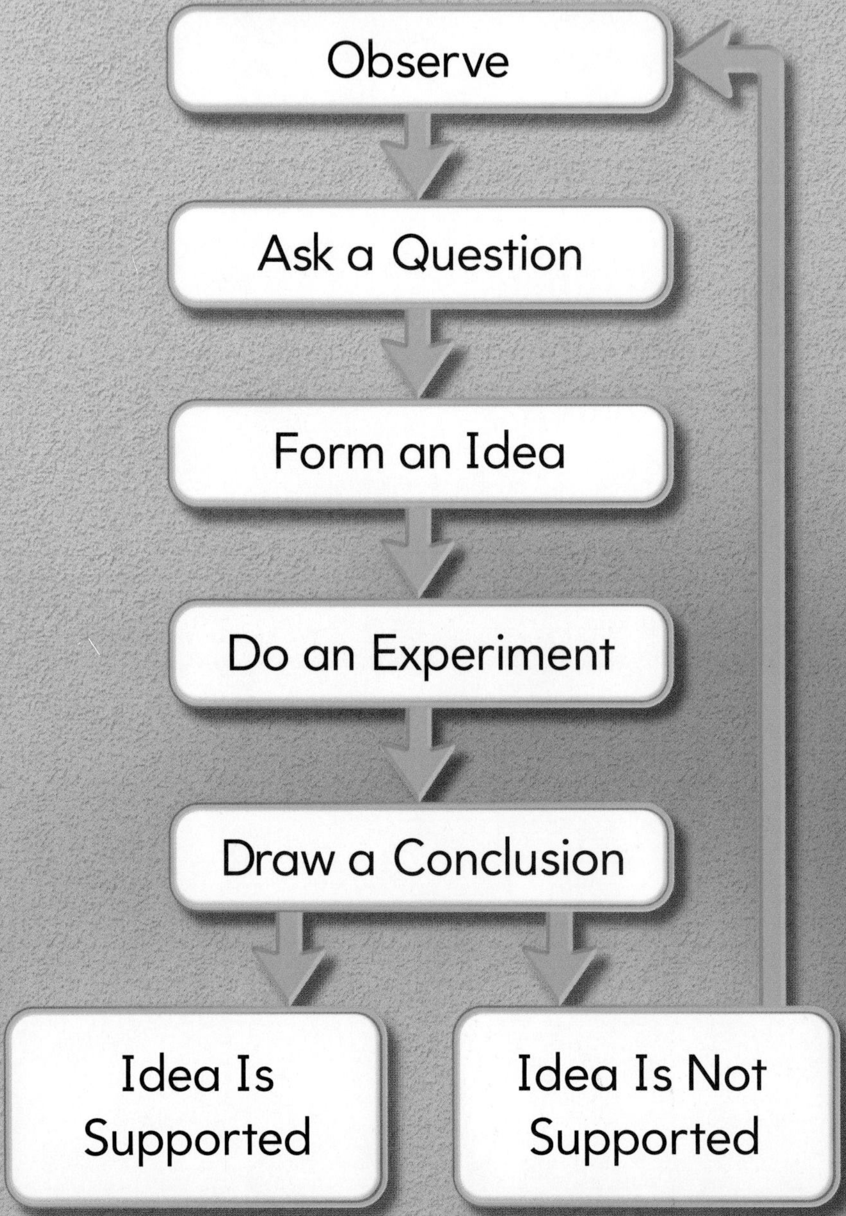

Observe

↓

Ask a Question

↓

Form an Idea

↓

Do an Experiment

↓

Draw a Conclusion

Idea Is Supported

Idea Is Not Supported

Try It Yourself!

Experiment With Bouncing Balls

Both balls look the same. However, one ball bounces and the other one does not.

1. What questions do you have about the balls?

2. How would you find out the answers?

3. Write an experiment plan. Tell what you think you will find out.

Be an Inventor

Lloyd French has enjoyed building things and taking them apart since sixth grade.

Mr. French invents robots. They are used as tools to make observations in places where people cannot easily go. One of his robots can travel to the bottom of the ocean. Another robot, called Cryobot, melts through thick layers of ice—either in Antarctica or on Mars. Cryobot takes photos as it moves through the ice.

"If you want to be a scientist or engineer, it helps to have a sense of curiosity and discovery."

What Is Technology?

The tools people make and use are all technology. A pencil is technology. A cryobot is technology. So is a robot that moves like a human.

Scientists use technology. For example, a microscope makes it possible to see things that cannot be seen with just the eyes. Measurement tools are used to make their observations more exact.

Many technologies make the world a better place to live. But sometimes solving one problem causes others. For example, airplanes make travel faster, but they are noisy and pollute the air.

A Better Idea

"I wish I had a better way to _____."
How would you fill in the blank?
Everyone wishes they could do something
more easily. Inventors try to make those
wishes come true. Inventing or improving
an invention takes time and patience.

Kids have been riding
on scooters for many
years. These newer
scooters are faster.
The tires won't get
flat. They are also
easier to carry from
place to place.

How to Be an Inventor

① **Find a problem.** It may be at school, at home, or in your community.

② **Think of a way to solve the problem.** List different ways to solve the problem. Decide which one will work best.

③ **Make a sample and try your invention.** Your idea may need many materials or none at all. Each time you try it, record how it works.

④ **Improve your invention.** Use what you learned to make your design better.

⑤ **Share your invention.** Draw or write about your invention. Tell how it makes an activity easier or more fun. If it did not work well, tell why.

Make Decisions

Plastic Litter and Ocean Animals

It is a windy day at the beach. A plastic bag blows out of sight. It may float in the ocean for years.

Plastic litter can harm ocean animals. Sometimes sea turtles mistake floating plastic bags for jellyfish, their favorite food. The plastic blocks the stomach, and food cannot get in. Pelicans and dolphins get tangled up in fishing line, six-pack rings, and packaging materials. Sometimes they get so tangled that they cannot move.

Deciding What to Do

How can ocean animals be protected from plastic litter?

Here's how to make your decision. You can use the same steps to help solve problems in your home, in your school, and in your community.

Learn → Learn about the problem. You could talk to an expert, read a science book, or explore a web site.

List → Make a list of actions you could take. Add actions other people could take.

Decide → Decide which action is best for you or your community.

Share → Explain your decision to others.

Science Safety

Know the safety rules of your classroom and follow them. Read and follow the safety tips in your science book.

- ▶ Wear safety goggles when your teacher tells you.

- ▶ Keep your work area clean. Tell your teacher about spills right away.

- ▶ Learn how to care for the plants and animals in your classroom.

- ▶ Wash your hands when you are done.

Earth Science

UNIT A

Earth Science

Reading in Science 2

Science in Georgia:
Earth Science Preview 4

Chapter 1
Weather Patterns 10

Chapter 2
Motions in the Sky 44

Independent Reading

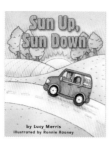

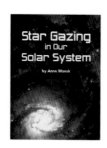

Sun Up,
Sun Down

Star Gazing
in Our Solar
System

Maria
Mitchell

Fun Facts

Azaleas are the first
flowers to bloom.
They are early signs
that spring is coming.

Earth Science

Changes in the sky can be observed throughout the year.

Azaleas bloom in Georgia

Start with a **Poem**

STANDARDS ELA2R3a. Reads a variety of texts and uses new words in oral and written language.

Storm

by Barbara Juster Esbensen

Day is night!
The world is black;
The thunder snaps
With a splitting crack!

Beaks of lightning
Rip the air
And willows swing
Their streaming hair.

Threads of rain
Bind earth to sky;
The gutter's torrent
Rushes by.

No house has shape,
No tree a form;
The town is lost
In summer storm!

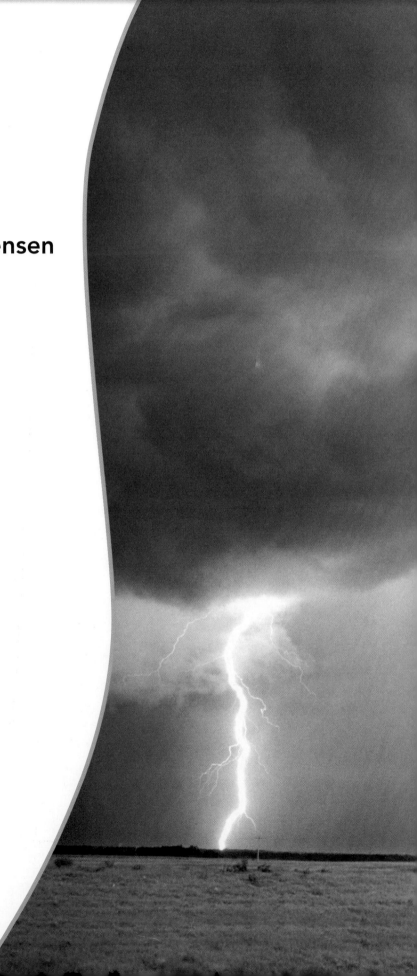

GPS STANDARDS S2E3a. Recognize effects that occur in a specific area caused by weather, plants, animals, and/or people.

What Changes in the Forest?

The Chattahoochee National Forest is thick with trees. But at one time it was not.

A Healthy Forest
Many trees grow tall and strong. Rich soil helps plants grow.

Timber!

In the past, people cut down trees in this forest for wood. Without trees, the soil became dry. Plants could not grow. Animals had to find new homes.

Fire!

When lightning strikes a tree, it can cause a forest fire. The fire can spread quickly from tree to tree.

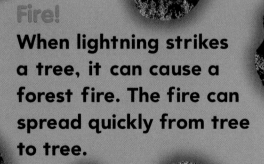

Science in Georgia

GPS STANDARDS S2E3a. Recognize effects that occur in a specific area caused by weather, plants, animals, and/or people.

Bad Bugs. Good Bugs.

People and fires are not the only things that can harm a forest. Tiny insects can harm and kill these large hemlock trees.

Bad Bugs!
Woolly adelgids harm hemlock trees. They suck fluid from a tree's needles. The tree becomes sick and can die.

A closer look at a woolly adelgid.

Good Bugs!
Scientists place these ladybird beetles on sick hemlock trees. The ladybird beetles eat the woolly adelgids. Then the trees can grow.

Choose a word to complete the sentence.

1. Ladybird beetles help trees by eating

(A) grasshoppers.

(B) leaves.

(C) woolly adelgids.

 Performance Task

How Do Plants Hold Soil?

Pour loose soil onto a sheet of paper. Then gently remove a plant from a pot, and place it on another sheet of paper. Fan the loose soil with paper. Then fan the plant's soil. What happened each time? Tell why.

7

Hands-On Project

GPS STANDARDS S2CS4b. Use models—such as a toy or a picture—to describe a feature of the primary thing. **GeorgiaTask S2E3B, S2E3D**

How Can School Grounds Change?

People and nature can cause Earth's land to change. Observe changes by studying the land around your school.

What You Need

- paper
- crayons or markers
- pencil

Step 1: Plan

- Choose an area of your school grounds to observe.

Step 2: Do It

- Draw a map of the area.

- Observe the area every day.

- Record the changes you observed.

Step 3: Share

- Share your observations with others.

- Were the changes caused by weather, plants, animals, or people? Were these changes helpful or harmful to the school grounds?

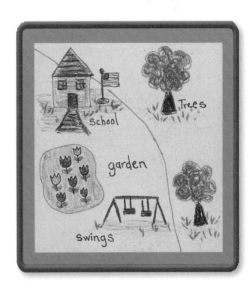

Chapter 1

Weather Patterns

Lesson Preview

LESSON 1

Weather changes all the time. Today it is cool and cloudy. Predict what the weather will be tomorrow.

LESSON 2

Winter in New York is cold and snowy. What is winter weather like where you live?

LESSON 3

Trees change each season. How do trees change in the summer?

Vocabulary Preview

Vocabulary

water cycle p. 18

evaporates p. 18

water vapor p. 18

condenses p. 19

precipitation p. 20

season p. 26

hibernate p. 37

migrate p. 37

Picture Glossary p. H18

Vocabulary Skill

Use Syllables

precipitation

Break the word apart into syllables. Say each syllable aloud, clapping once for each syllable.

migrate

Some animals migrate, or move to warmer places in fall.

condenses

Water vapor condenses, or changes to drops of water.

precipitation

Water that falls from clouds is called precipitation.

hibernate

Some animals hibernate, or go into a deep sleep.

Georgia
Performance Standards

Start with Your Standards

Habits of Mind

S2CS2a. Use whole numbers in ordering, counting, identifying, measuring, and describing things and experiences.

S2CS3a. Use ordinary hand tools and instruments to construct, measure, and look at objects.

Earth Science

S2E2c. Relate the length of day and night to the change in seasons (for example: Days are longer than the night in the summer.).

S2E3a. Recognize effects that occur in a specific area caused by weather, plants, animals, and/or people.

Lesson 1

GPS GEORGIA STANDARDS

S2CS3a. Use ordinary hand tools and instruments to construct, measure, and look at objects.
S2E3a. Recognize effects that occur in a specific area caused by weather, plants, animals, and/or people.

Essential ? Question How Does Weather Change?

Science and You

When the weather changes, you may need to change your plans for the day.

Inquiry Skill

Use Numbers You can use numbers to compare temperatures.

What You Need

thermometer

Daily and Weekly Weather					
	Monday	Tuesday	Wednesday	Thursday	Friday
Morning					
	Temperature___°F	Temperature___°F	Temperature___°F	Temperature___°F	Temperature___°F
Midday					
	Temperature___°F	Temperature___°F	Temperature___°F	Temperature___°F	Temperature___°F
Afternoon					
	Temperature___°F	Temperature___°F	Temperature___°F	Temperature___°F	Temperature___°F

weather chart

Compare Weather

Steps

1. **Observe** See whether it is sunny, cloudy, raining, or snowing. Record what you see.

2. **Measure** Find the outdoor temperature. Record your findings.

3. **Use Numbers** Repeat steps 1 and 2 two more times during the day. Compare the temperatures you recorded.

4. Repeat steps 1–3 for a week.

STEP 1

STEP 2

STEP 3

Think and Share

1. What changes did you observe during any one day?

2. **Infer** What can you infer about morning temperatures?

Guided Inquiry

Experiment Make a plan to measure rainfall. Talk with others about your findings.

Vocabulary

water cycle

evaporates

water vapor

condenses

precipitation

▶ **Reading Skill**

Main Idea and Details

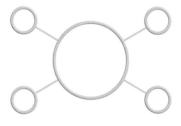

GPS S2E3a. Recognize effects that occur in a specific area caused by weather, plants, animals and/or people.

Daily Weather Patterns

Weather changes in patterns over time. Weather can change from day to day. Weather can also change during a day.

The air is often warmer in the afternoon than it is in the morning. The Sun warms the air during the day. Then the air gets cooler again at night. These changes in temperature are measured with a thermometer.

a lightning storm

Sudden Changes

Sometimes weather can change very quickly. It might be a calm and clear day. Then a storm comes, bringing rain, thunder, and lightning in the afternoon. Lightning can cause fires. Heavy rains can cause flooding.

Scientists called meteorologists use tools to study the weather. They tell what kind of weather is coming. They use radar to keep track of weather changes.

▶ **Main Idea** How might weather change during a day?

This radar map shows rain in the Georgia area.

■ no rain   ■ light rain   ■ heavy rain

Atlanta

The Water Cycle

Heat from the Sun warms land, water, and air. The Sun's heat causes water to change form and move. Water moving from Earth to the air and back again is called the **water cycle**.

▶ **Main Idea** How does the Sun change water?

2

Water as a gas is called **water vapor**. You cannot see it. It mixes into the air.

1

The Sun warms the water. The water **evaporates**, or changes to a gas.

3 Air with water vapor rises into cooler air. Water vapor **condenses**, or changes to drops of water. These drops of water form clouds.

4 As the drops get bigger, they get heavier. The drops fall to the ground as rain, snow, sleet, or hail.

5 Rain and melted snow collect in streams, rivers, lakes, and oceans. The water cycle begins again.

Express Lab

Activity Card 1
See the Wind Move

Precipitation and Wind

Water that falls from clouds is called **precipitation**. Rain, snow, sleet, and hail are kinds of precipitation. When the air is warm, rain falls. When the air is cold enough, snow may fall. If falling snow melts and refreezes, it changes to sleet. When falling rain is tossed about in cold air, it freezes into balls of ice. These balls of ice are called hail. Hail often forms during thunderstorms.

◄ hail

Strong wind can damage trees. ▼

**snowstorm
with drifts**

Wind is moving air. Wind can be gentle, or it can be very strong. During many storms, a strong wind blows. Strong wind can blow falling rain or snow. Wind can blow fallen snow into drifts.

▶ **Main Idea** **What are two different kinds of precipitation?**

Lesson Wrap-Up

❶ **Vocabulary** What happens to water when the Sun heats it?

❷ **Reading Skill** What happens to water in the water cycle?

❸ **Use Numbers** A morning temperature is 50°F. What might an afternoon temperature be?

Technology Visit **www.eduplace.com/gascp** to find out more about weather.

GPS STANDARDS S2E3a. Recognize effects that occur in a specific area caused by weather, plants, animals, and/or people.

Take Cover!

Flash, crash, rumble! Lightning creates the thunder that gives thunderstorms their special name.

Lightning is a giant spark of electricity. Sometimes dangerous tornadoes are formed from thunderstorms. A tornado is a very strong wind that twists in a circle as it moves. Tornadoes have the fastest winds on Earth — sometimes reaching over 300 miles per hour!

▲ In the spring and summer, Georgia has thunderstorms like this. When you hear thunder, it's time to go inside to be safe!

Lesson 2

GPS GEORGIA STANDARDS

S2CS2a. Use whole numbers in ordering, counting, identifying, measuring, and describing things and experiences.

S2E2c. Relate the length of day and night to the change in seasons (for example: Days are longer than the night in the summer.).

Essential Question

What Is the Pattern of the Seasons?

Science and You

Knowing the pattern of the seasons helps you know the best time to plant seeds.

Inquiry Skill

Communicate You can communicate by talking to others about what you find out.

What You Need

goggles

water and soil

2 thermometers

Measure Heat

Steps

STEP 1

1. Put the cups of soil and water in a refrigerator overnight.

2. **Measure** Remove the cups from the refrigerator. Measure and record the temperature of each material.

STEP 2

3. **Record Data** Put the cups in a warm, sunny place for 20 minutes. Record the temperature of each material again.

STEP 3

Think and Share

1. **Communicate** Tell how the temperature of each material changed.

2. **Infer** The thermometers measured the amount of heat absorbed. What was the source of heat?

Guided Inquiry

Ask Questions Think about other times when the temperatures of materials might change. What questions would you ask?

Learn by Reading

GPS **S2E2c.** Relate the length of day and night to the change in seasons (for example: Days are longer than the night in the summer.).

Weather Patterns of the Seasons

A **season** is a time of year. Winter, spring, summer, and fall are the four seasons. They occur in this order every year. Each season has its own weather pattern.

Air temperatures change with the seasons. Winter is the coolest. Summer is the warmest. In spring, temperatures slowly rise. In fall, temperatures slowly fall.

Compare the thermometers. How is the winter temperature different in these places?

Bismarck, North Dakota

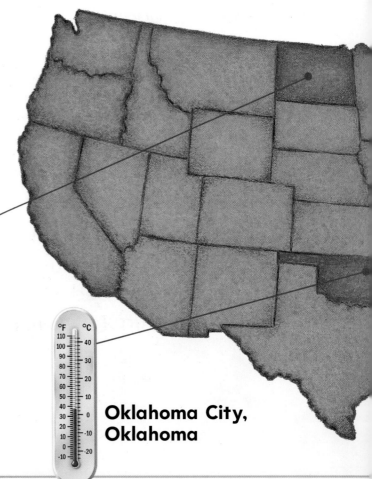

Oklahoma City, Oklahoma

Weather patterns are different from place to place. In some places, winter weather is very cold. In other places, winters are just a little cooler than summers. Some places have about the same amount of precipitation in all four seasons. In other places, one season is very wet and the others are dry.

▶ **Sequence** How do temperatures change as the seasons change?

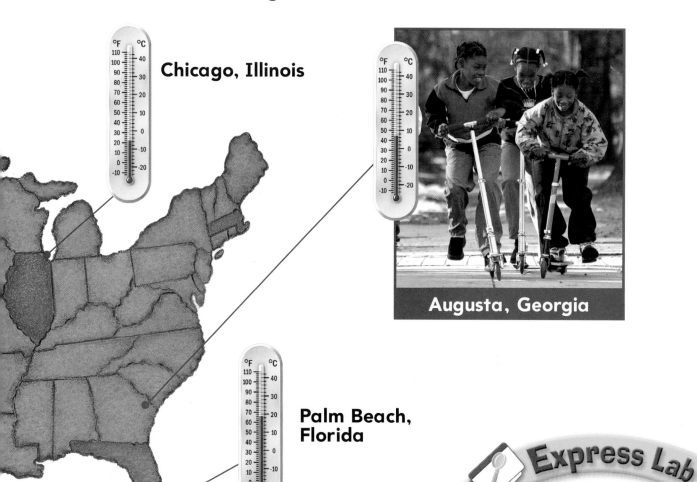

Chicago, Illinois

Augusta, Georgia

Palm Beach, Florida

Express Lab

Activity Card 2
Compare the Weather

winter

Winter days have the fewest hours of daylight.

spring

In spring, daytime slowly gets longer.

Daylight Patterns

The Sun shines in the daytime. The number of daylight hours changes with the seasons. This pattern of changing daylight repeats every year.

The Sun warms Earth's land and water. Heat moves from the land and water into the air.

The land, air, and water get warmer when there are more hours of daylight. This is why summer has the warmest weather.

summer

Summer days have the most hours of daylight.

fall

In fall, the daytime slowly gets shorter.

▶ **Sequence** How does the number of daylight hours change as the seasons change?

Lesson Wrap-Up

❶ **Vocabulary** What is a **season**?

❷ **Reading Skill** Which season comes after the one with the most daylight hours?

❸ **Communicate** Tell why summer has the warmest weather.

💻 **Technology** Visit **www.eduplace.com/gascp** to find out more about seasons.

STAYING SAFE IN THE SUN

In summer, there are more daylight hours. Too much sunlight is not healthful. It can harm your skin and damage your eyes.

You need to protect your skin and eyes from the Sun's rays in all seasons. The Sun's rays are strongest midday. If you must be outdoors at that time, try to stay in the shade. Cover your skin with tightly woven, lightweight clothing.

The Sun's rays can be harmful even when it is cold outdoors. The Sun's light can reflect off snow.

How is this child keeping safe in the Sun?

GPS STANDARDS S2E2c. Relate the length of day and night to the change in seasons (for example: Days are longer than the night in the summer.).

SOCIAL STUDIES **LINK**

Safety in the Sun

Wear sunscreen to protect your skin. Put it on before you go outdoors.	
Wear a hat with a brim to protect your neck, ears, and face.	
Wear sunglasses to protect your eyes.	
You sweat more in warmer weather. Drink a lot of water to replace the water you lose.	

Sharing Ideas

1. **Write About It** Make a list of things you do outdoors in warm weather. Write about how you can stay safe.

2. **Talk About It** Talk with your classmates about Sun safety at school. Make a class list of ways to keep safe while outdoors.

GEORGIA STANDARDS

S2CS3a. Use ordinary hand tools and instruments to construct, measure, and look at objects.

S2L1b. Relate seasonal changes to observations of how a tree changes throughout a school year.

Essential Question ? How Do Living Things Change With the Seasons?

Science and You

Knowing how living things change with the seasons helps you know when you might see baby animals.

Inquiry Skill

Compare Tell how objects are alike or different.

What You Need

2 cups and 2 bags

2 thermometers

ice cubes

different fabrics

Compare Fabrics

Steps

STEP 1

1. Put an ice cube in each bag. Wrap a piece of fabric around each bag.

2. Place a fabric-wrapped bag in each cup. Slide a thermometer into each cup as shown.

STEP 2

3. **Compare** Wait 15 minutes. Compare the temperatures on the thermometers. Record what you observe.

STEP 3

Think and Share

1. Heat moved from the air through the fabric and into the ice. Which fabric kept the air warmer?

2. **Infer** Which fabric would be good to wear in cold weather? Tell why.

Guided Inquiry

Be an Inventor Make a container to keep ice from melting. Tell about the materials you would use.

▶ **Vocabulary**

hibernate

migrate

▶ **Reading Skill**
Compare and
Contrast

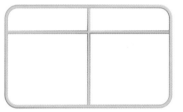

GPS **S2L1b.** Relate seasonal changes to
observations of how a tree changes
throughout a school year.

Plants and the Seasons

Changes in the seasons cause plants to change. Plants change as the air slowly warms or cools. They change as the number of daylight hours changes.

Changes with the Seasons

Season	spring
How a Sweet Gum Tree Changes	 Leaves grow and flowers bloom.

Activity Card 3
Show Changes

34

In spring, many plants flower. In summer, the fruits grow. Some plants have leaves that change color in fall. Where winters are very cold, plants stop growing.

▶ **Compare and Contrast** How are plants different in spring and summer?

summer	fall	winter
Spiny fruits form. Seeds form inside the fruits.	Leaves turn red and fall. Seeds spread.	Leaves and most of the fruits have fallen. The seeds rest.

Animals and the Seasons

Animals change with the seasons. Some change how they look. Most change what they do. The fur of some animals gets thicker in the fall and stays thick all winter. The fur may change color, too.

In fall, the antlers are fully grown. The deer's fur gets thicker.

In spring, a male deer's antlers begin to grow.

It is hard for animals to find food in winter. Some animals collect food in fall to store for winter. Other animals **hibernate**, or go into a deep sleep. In spring, they come out of hibernation. They find food and have their young.

▲ Ground squirrels hibernate in winter.

Some animals **migrate**, or move to warmer places in fall. The animals can find food in these warm places.

▲ A ground squirrel comes out of its burrow in spring.

▶ **Compare and Contrast** How are a deer's antlers different in spring and fall?

Some monarch butterflies migrate in fall.

Dressing for the Seasons

People change the things they do with the seasons. As the weather changes, people wear different clothes.

A hat helps keep in body heat.

Layers of clothes keep heat near your body.

Socks and sturdy shoes keep your feet warm and dry.

Lesson Wrap-Up

❶ **Vocabulary** What do animals do when they **hibernate**?

❷ **Reading Skill** Tell how a plant is different in two seasons.

❸ **Compare** Tell how an animal is different in two seasons.

💻 **Technology** Visit **www.eduplace.com/gascp** to find out more about living in seasons.

STANDARDS S2CS6d. All different kinds of people can be and are scientists.

Meteorologist

Meteorologists study the weather. They explain today's weather. They predict the weather for tomorrow. That helps people be ready when storms come.

What It Takes!

- A college degree in science
- An interest in weather and people

STANDARDS S2CS2a. Use whole numbers in ordering, counting, identifying, measuring, and describing things and experiences. **M2N2a.** Correctly add and subtract two whole numbers up to three digits each with regrouping. **ELA2W1b.** Use traditional organizational patterns for conveying information (e.g., chronological order, similarity and difference, answering questions).

Math Read a Chart

The chart shows weather data for the spring months in Savannah, Georgia.

Weather in Savannah, Georgia			
	April	May	June
Rain	3 inches	4 inches	6 inches
Temperature	66°F	74°F	78°F
Clear Days	7	7	8
Cloudy Days	12	11	11

1. Tell about the weather in May.

2. How many degrees warmer is it in June than it is in May?

 **Winter Differences**

Kayla lives in Florida. Jason lives in Illinois. Write how winter is different in these two places. Write about winter where you live.

GeorgiaTask S2E2D

When do the number of daylight hours change?

- Each month, choose one day. Find out what time the sun rises and sets for each of these days.

- Write the number of daylight hours for these days on a calendar.

- Use your calendar. Find the days with the most and least hours of daylight.

Visual Summary

Weather, plants, and animals change with the seasons.

Patterns of Change

Season	Winter	Spring	Summer	Fall
Temperature	coolest	slowly rises	warmest	slowly falls
Plants				
Animals				

Main Ideas

1. Which season has the longest days? **(p. 28)** `S2E2c`

2. Why does water evaporate? **(p. 18)** `S2E3a`

3. How do some plants change in the winter? **(p. 35)** `S2L1b`

4. What do animals do in fall to get ready for winter? **(pp. 36–37)** `S2E3a`

Vocabulary

Choose the correct word from the box.

5. A time of year

6. When water vapor changes to drops of water

7. Water that falls from clouds

8. Water moving from Earth to the air and back again

S2CS7a

water cycle
(p. 18)

condenses
(p. 19)

precipitation
(p. 20)

season (p. 26)

Using Science Skills

9. **Compare** Draw the same tree or plant in winter and spring. How are the drawings alike and different?

S2E2c

10. **Critical Thinking** Why would a place have fewer hours of daylight in fall than in summer?

S2E2c

GPS CRCT Prep

Choose a word to complete the sentence.

11. The sweet gum tree flowers in the spring because the days are

longer.   shorter.   colder.

              S2L1b

Chapter 2

Motions in the Sky

LESSON 1

The night sky is filled with many objects. What can you see in the night sky?

LESSON 2

My shadow was short. Now it is long. What causes this to happen?

LESSON 3

There was a full Moon last week. What will the Moon look like tonight?

LESSON 4

You can see many twinkling stars on a clear night. Do they all look the same?

Vocabulary Preview

Vocabulary

Sun p. 50

solar system p. 52

planet p. 52

rotates p. 58

revolve p. 60

orbit p. 60

Moon p. 68

phases p. 70

star p. 76

constellation p. 78

Picture Glossary p. H18

Vocabulary Skill

Classify Words

solar system

The solar system is made up of different objects. Say the names of each object.

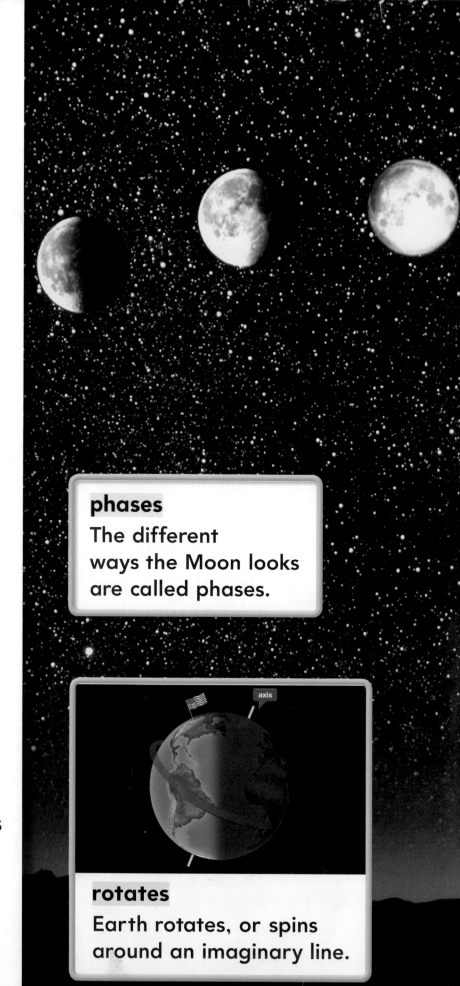

phases
The different ways the Moon looks are called phases.

rotates
Earth rotates, or spins around an imaginary line.

Start with Your Standards

Habits of Mind

S2CS4b. Use a model—such as a toy or a picture—to describe a feature of the primary thing.

S2CS4c. Describe changes in the size, weight, color, or movement of things, and note which of their other qualities remain the same during a specific change.

Nature of Science

S2CS7c. Tools such as thermometers, rulers, and balances often give more information about things than can be obtained by just observing things without help.

Earth Science

S2E1a. Describe the physical attributes of stars—size, brightness, and patterns.

S2E2a. Investigate the position of the sun in relation to a fixed object on earth at various times of the day.

S2E2b. Determine how the shadows change through the day by making a shadow stick or using a sundial.

S2E2d. Use observations and charts to record the shape of the moon for a period of time.

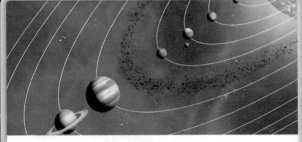

solar system

The Sun and the space objects that move around it make up our solar system.

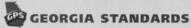
GEORGIA STANDARDS

S2CS7c. Tools such as thermometers, rulers, and balances often give more information about things than can be obtained by just observing things without help.

S2E1a. Describe the physical attributes of stars—size, brightness, and patterns.

Essential Question

What Makes Up the Solar System?

Science and You

Knowing about the solar system helps you see how important the Sun is to the planets.

Inquiry Skill

Predict Use what you observe and know to tell what you think will happen.

What You Need

2 thermometers

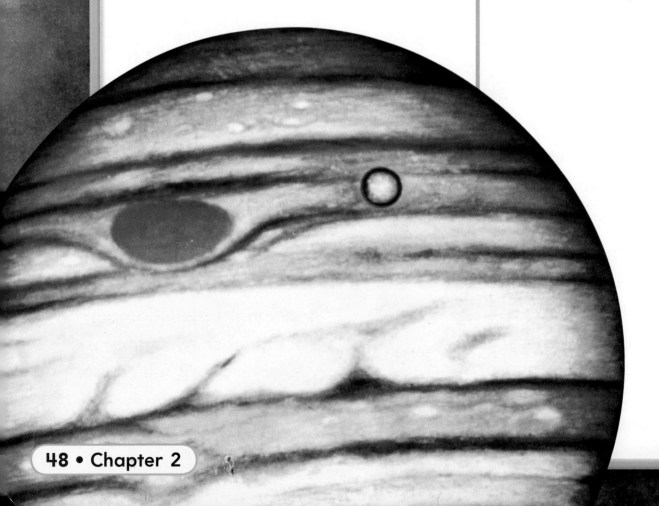

Light and Heat

Steps

1. Put one thermometer in a sunny place. Put the other thermometer in a shaded place.

2. **Predict** Record the temperature shown on each thermometer. Predict how the temperatures will change.

3. **Record Data** Wait 15 minutes. Record the temperatures again.

STEP 1

STEP 2

	First Time	Second Time
Sun	_____ °F	_____ °F
Shade	_____ °F	_____ °F

Think and Share

1. How did what you observed compare to what you predicted?

2. **Infer** How did the temperatures change? Tell why.

STEP 3

Guided Inquiry

Experiment Do the activity a few more times. Compare your findings. Were they the same each time? Tell why or why not.

▶ **Vocabulary**

Sun

solar system

planet

▶ **Reading Skill**
**Main Idea
and Details**

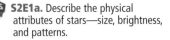

GPS **S2E1a.** Describe the physical
attributes of stars—size, brightness,
and patterns.

The Sun

The **Sun** is the brightest
object in the day sky. The Sun
is much larger than Earth. It
looks small because it is very
far away. The Sun is made of
hot gases that give off energy.
The Sun's energy reaches Earth
as light. Some of this light is
changed to heat.

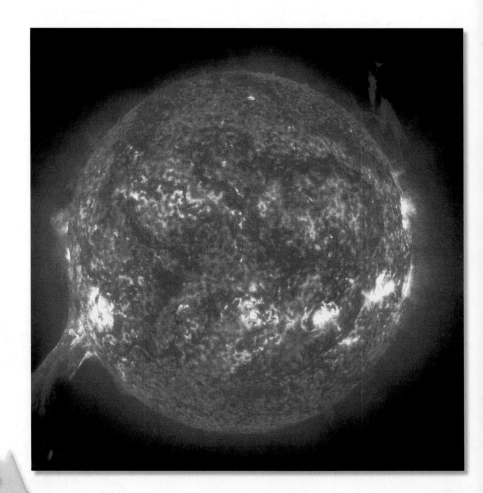

Living things on Earth use energy from the Sun. Land, air, and water are warmed by the Sun. The Sun keeps people and animals warm. Light from the Sun helps people and animals see. It helps plants live and grow.

▶ **Main Idea** How do living things use energy from the Sun?

Plants use the Sun's light to make their own food.

The rocks are warmed by the Sun's heat.

The Solar System

The Sun and the space objects that move around it make up our **solar system**. There are eight planets in our solar system. A **planet** is a large object that moves around the Sun. Planets are always in the sky. Many planets have moons. Earth is a planet with one moon.

▶ **Main Idea** What makes up the solar system?

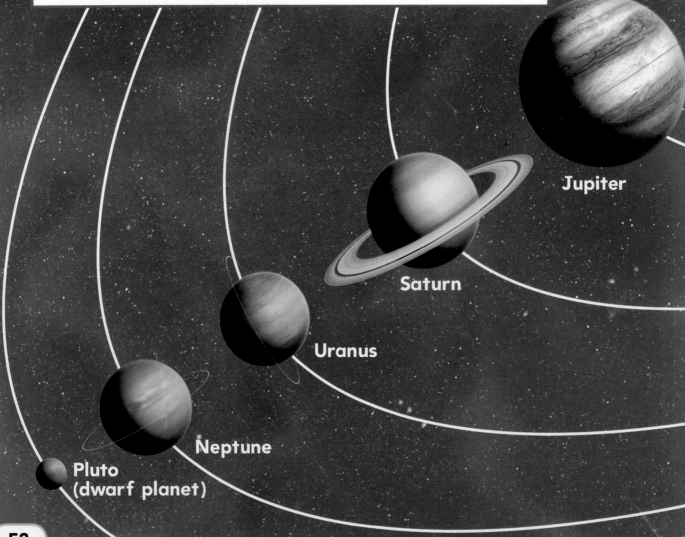

Jupiter

Saturn

Uranus

Neptune

Pluto
(dwarf planet)

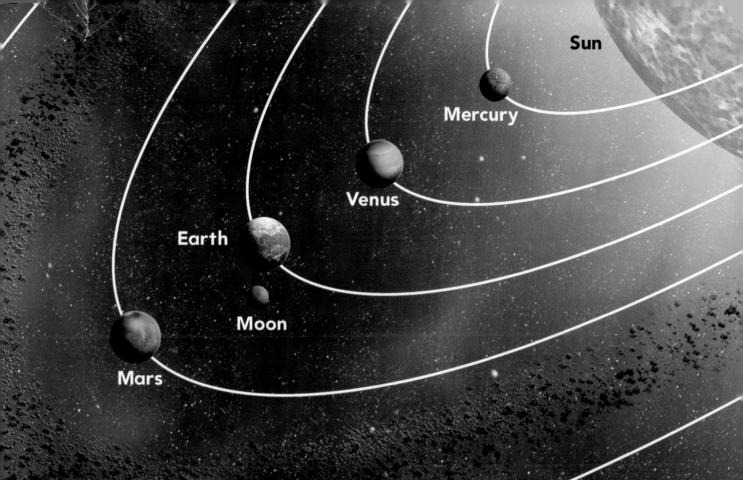

Sun

Mercury

Venus

Earth

Moon

Mars

Lesson Wrap-Up

1 Vocabulary What is a **planet**?

2 Reading Skill How do living things use the Sun's energy?

3 Predict What might happen to a plant if it did not get enough light from the Sun? Tell why.

Technology Visit **www.eduplace.com/gascp** to find out more about the Sun.

Orion's Surprise

Where can you find the glowing swirl shown here? It's in the night sky, in the constellation called Orion, the Hunter. Orion is a winter constellation. On clear winter nights you can see it in the southern sky from anywhere north of the equator.

The colorful swirl is made of gas and dust. To find it, look for three bright stars of Orion's belt. Then find the points that make up the sword. The middle spot in the sword is the swirl.

Orion's Sword
Scientists use a powerful telescope to see the bright colors of Orion.

GEORGIA STANDARDS

S2CS4c. Describe changes in the size, weight, color, or movement of things, and note which of their other qualities remain the same during a specific change.
S2E2b. Determine how the shadows change through the day by making a shadow stick or using a sundial.

Essential Question

How Does Earth Move?

Science and You

Knowing how Earth moves helps you understand day and night.

Inquiry Skill

Observe Use your senses to find out about something.

What You Need

large sheet of paper

marker

ruler

Observe Shadows

Steps

STEP 1

1. Go outdoors. Place a large sheet of paper on the ground. Make an X in the center of it.

2. **Observe** Hold the ruler as shown. Trace its shadow. Write the time.

STEP 2

3. Put an arrow on your drawing to show where the Sun is in the sky. **Safety:** Do not look right at the Sun!

4. Repeat steps 2 and 3 two more times during the day.

STEP 3

Think and Share

1. How did the length and position of the shadow change during the day?

2. **Infer** What caused the shadow to change?

Guided Inquiry

Work Together Work with a partner. Use a flashlight and different objects to make shadows. Discuss what materials make shadows. Tell how the shadows change.

Vocabulary

rotates

revolve

orbit

Reading Skill

Draw Conclusions

S2E2a. Investigate the position of the sun in relation to a fixed object on earth at various times of the day.

Earth Spins

Each day the Sun seems to move across the sky. But the Sun does not move. Earth **rotates**, or spins around an imaginary line. The line is called an axis. It takes Earth 24 hours, or one day, to rotate one time.

As Earth rotates, different parts face the Sun. When the part where you live faces the Sun, you have day. When the part where you live faces away from the Sun, you have night.

Where is it day in this picture?

axis

Shadows Change

Light from the Sun shines on Earth. Shadows form when an object blocks sunlight. As Earth rotates, shadows change length and position. People can tell time by observing the Sun and shadows.

morning

In the morning, the Sun is low in the sky. Shadows are long. They grow shorter and shorter until noon.

noon

At about noon, the Sun is at its highest point in the sky. Shadows are shortest.

afternoon

In the afternoon, the Sun is low in the sky again. Shadows grow longer.

▶ **Draw Conclusions** When is your shadow its shortest?

Express Lab

Activity Card 5
Change Shadows by Using a Flashlight

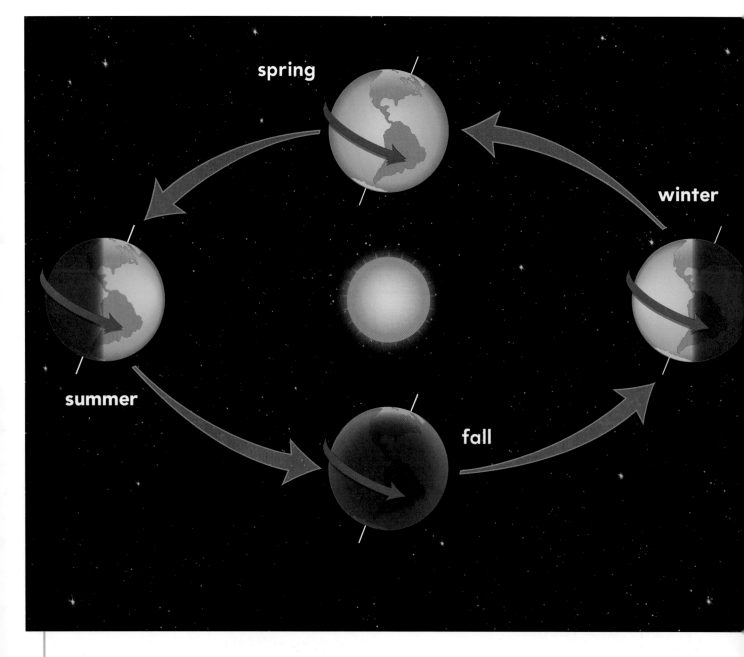

Earth Moves Around the Sun

While Earth rotates, it also moves in another way. Earth and the other planets **revolve**, or move in a path, around the Sun. The path that one space object travels around another is called an **orbit**. It takes one year for Earth to revolve around the Sun.

During Earth's orbit, the seasons change. When our part of Earth is tilted toward the Sun, we get more direct light from the Sun. It is summer. As Earth revolves around the Sun, our part of Earth tilts away from the Sun. Sunlight hits our part of Earth on a slant, so we get less light. Then it is winter.

▶ **Draw Conclusions If it is spring, how long will it be until it is spring again?**

Lesson Wrap-Up

❶ **Vocabulary** Which of Earth's movements takes one year?

❷ **Reading Skill** When the United States has night, where is it day?

❸ **Observe** What happens to shadows throughout the day?

💻 **Technology** Visit **www.eduplace.com/gascp** to find out more about Earth's movements.

A Shadow Fable

Why do shadows change during the day? In this fable, three animals learn the answer.

7 am

Cast

Narrator
Squirrel
Bulldog
Panther
Wise Owl

STANDARDS S2E2b. Determine how the shadows change through the day by making a shadow stick or using a sundial.

READING LINK

Narrator: At 7 o'clock on a sunny morning, three animals meet in a field.

Squirrel: My goodness, I must have grown. Look at how tall I am.

Bulldog: Why do you say that, Squirrel?

Squirrel: Don't you see how long my shadow is? That must mean that I am very tall.

Panther: Ha, look! My shadow is even longer than yours!

Squirrel: We must be the tallest animals in the world.

Narrator: Five hours later standing in the same spot, they noticed many changes.

Panther: Hey, what happened to my shadow? Now it's short! Am I getting shorter? Am I shrinking?

Bulldog: You don't look shorter to me.

Squirrel: Then who shrank our shadows? Was it you, Narrator?

Narrator: No, of course not. Look and see what happens at 5 o'clock that afternoon, standing in the same spot.

Bulldog: Look, now our shadows are very long again!

Panther: But they point in a different direction than they did this morning. How strange!

Wise Owl (from a tree above): Excuse me. Don't you know about the Sun?

All: The Sun? What do you mean?

Wise Owl: Our bodies make shadows because they block the Sun's light.

Squirrel: I know that early in the morning, the Sun rises in the east.

Wise Owl: Yes! Shadows are long when the Sun is low in the sky.

Bulldog: What happens as the Sun climbs higher in the sky?

5 pm

Wise Owl: The shadows become shorter. They are shortest at 12 o'clock noon. As the Sun sets shadows grow long again.

Narrator: Wise Owl, how did you learn so much about shadows?

Wise Owl: By studying in science class!

Sharing Ideas

1. **Write About It** When are shadows longest? When are they shortest? Answer with pictures and words.

2. **Talk About It** What can you learn by studying the shadow of an object?

GPS GEORGIA STANDARDS

S2CS4b. Use a model—such as a toy or a picture—to describe a feature of the primary thing.
S2E2d. Use observations and charts to record the shape of the moon for a period of time.

Essential Question

How Does the Moon Move?

Science and You

Knowing how the Moon moves helps you understand why it looks different each night.

Inquiry Skill

Use Models Use a model to learn about the Moon.

What You Need

lamp

Moon model

Moon chart

Moon Phases

Steps

1. **Use Models** Place a lamp on a table in a darkened room. The lamp is the Sun. One child sits in a chair as Earth. One child holds a model Moon.

2. **Observe** The Moon slowly walks around Earth. Earth observes the changes in the amount of light on the Moon.

3. **Record Data** On the Moon chart, Earth records how the light and shadows on the Moon model change.

Think and Share

1. When did you see most of the Moon model?

2. What happened to the Moon model as it moved around the Earth model? Tell why.

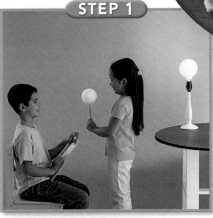

STEP 1

STEP 2

STEP 3

Guided Inquiry

Work Together Switch roles so that everyone has a turn to be Earth. Compare your results. Talk about how the Moon seemed to change.

► **Vocabulary**

Moon

phases

► **Reading Skill**

Cause and Effect

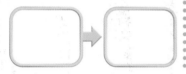

GPS **S2E2d.** Use observations and charts to record the shape of the moon for a period of time.

The Moon

The **Moon** is a large sphere made of rock. It is the closest large space object to Earth. As Earth rotates, the Moon seems to move across the sky at night. From Earth, you can see dark spots on the Moon. With a telescope, you can see mountains and pits, or craters, on the Moon.

Earth can be seen from the Moon.

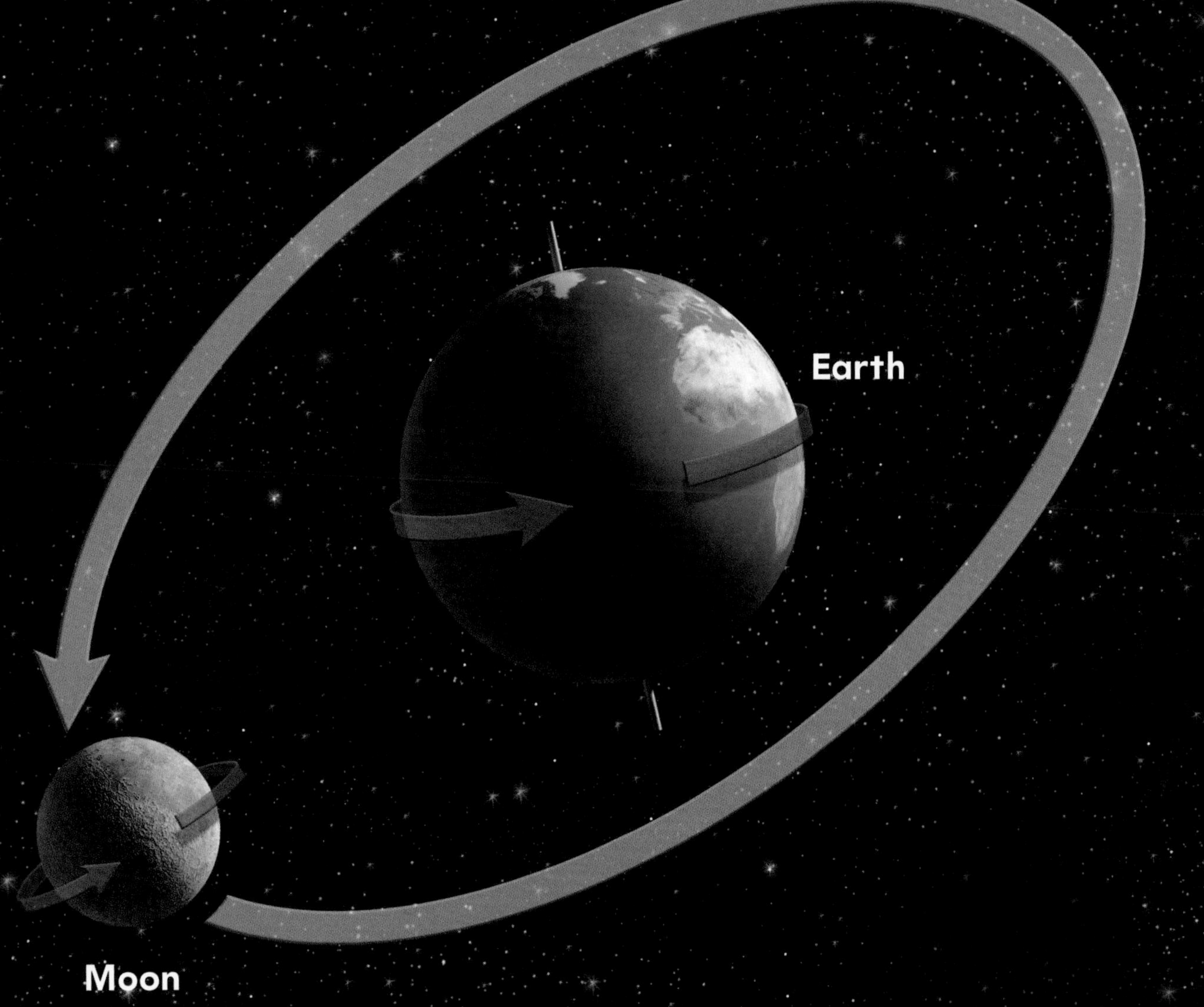

Earth

Moon

The Moon in Motion

It takes about one month for the Moon to revolve around Earth. This pattern repeats every month.

▶ **Cause and Effect** Why does the Moon seem to move across the sky?

Express Lab

Activity Card 6
Show Phases of the Moon

first quarter

new

The Changing Moon

The Moon does not have its own light. It reflects the Sun's light. The Sun shines on only one side of the Moon at a time. As the Moon revolves around Earth, you may see only a part of the Moon's lighted side. The Moon looks a little different every night. The different ways the Moon looks are called **phases**. The phases repeat every four weeks.

▶ **Cause and Effect** What causes the phases of the Moon?

full

last quarter

new

Lesson Wrap-Up

❶ **Vocabulary** What is the **Moon**?

❷ **Reading Skill** Why does the Moon look bright in the night sky?

❸ **Use Models** How does using models help you understand real objects?

Technology Visit **www.eduplace.com/gascp** to find out more about the Moon.

Long ago, people made up stories about dark spots that they saw on the Moon. Compare one story to the facts.

The Tale of Rabbit and Coyote

by Tony Johnston
illustrated by Tomie dePaola

Now Rabbit knew of a ladder that reached into the sky. He began to climb it. Up, up, up. And he hopped all the way to the moon.

Then he hid the ladder.

Far below, he saw Coyote looking for him up in the sky. But try as he might, Coyote never found the ladder.

That is why, to this day, Coyote sits gazing at the moon.

And now and then he howls at it. For he is still *very* furious with Rabbit.

THE TALE OF
RABBIT AND
COYOTE

Tony Johnston • Tomie dePaola

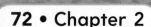

GPS **STANDARDS S2CS5a.** Describe and compare things in terms of number, shape, texture, size, weight, color, and motion.

READING **LINK**

The Sun and Moon

by Patrick Moore
illustration by Paul Doherty

When you look at the moon, you can see bright and dark patches. The dark patches are called seas, but they are not real seas; there is no water in them and in fact there is no water anywhere on the moon. There are high mountains, and there are many craters, which are really holes with walls around them.

The
Sun
and
Moon

Patrick Moore

Sharing Ideas

1. **Write About It** Write a story to tell why you think there are dark spots on the Moon.

2. **Talk About It** Why do you think people made up stories about what they saw in the Moon?

 **GEORGIA STANDARDS**

S2CS4b. Use a model—such as a toy or a picture—to describe a feature of the primary thing.
S2E1a. Describe the physical attributes of stars—size, brightness, and patterns.

Essential Question: What Stars Can You See?

Science and You

Constellations can help you remember where some stars are in the sky.

Inquiry Skill

Compare Tell how objects or events are alike or different.

What You Need

black paper

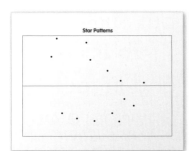

star patterns

cardboard

pencil and tape

Star Pictures

Steps

1 Place one half of the black paper over the cardboard. Place a star pattern over that half of the black paper.

STEP 1

2 **Use Models** Make the star pattern on the black paper. Punch a hole for each dot.

STEP 2

3 Repeat steps 1 and 2 for the other star pattern. Tape the black paper to a window.

Think and Share

1. What pictures did you see?

2. **Compare** How are the star patterns alike and different?

STEP 3

Guided Inquiry

Experiment At night, go outdoors with an adult. Draw the stars that you see. Point out the brighter stars. Then look for star patterns. Share your drawings.

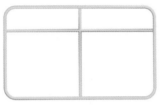
Stars

A **star** is a big ball of hot gases that gives off light. Stars are always in the sky. The Sun is a star. The Sun is the closest star to Earth. That is why living things on Earth are able to use the Sun's energy. The Sun's light is so bright that you cannot see any other stars during the day.

Stars are different colors. The Sun is a yellow star.

blue star

red star

Express Lab

Activity Card 7
Make a Constellation

76

At night, when our side of Earth faces away from the Sun, the sky is dark. Then you can see the other stars. They look like tiny points of light. There are so many that they are hard to count. Like the Sun, the other stars are very large. They look much smaller because they are farther away than the Sun. Some stars look brighter than others. Those stars may be bigger, hotter, or closer to Earth.

▶ **Compare and Contrast** How are all stars alike?

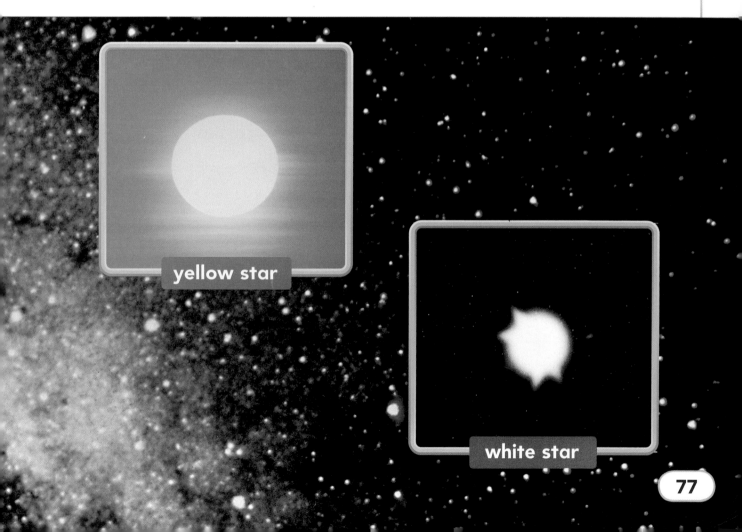

yellow star

white star

Star Patterns

Some stars seem to form pictures.
A **constellation** is a group of stars that
forms a picture. People have named the
constellations. Constellations can help you
find some stars. The star Polaris is in the
Little Dipper. Polaris is also called the North
Star. Sailors can use the North Star to help
them guide their ships.

▶ **Compare and Contrast** What are two
groups of stars that look alike?

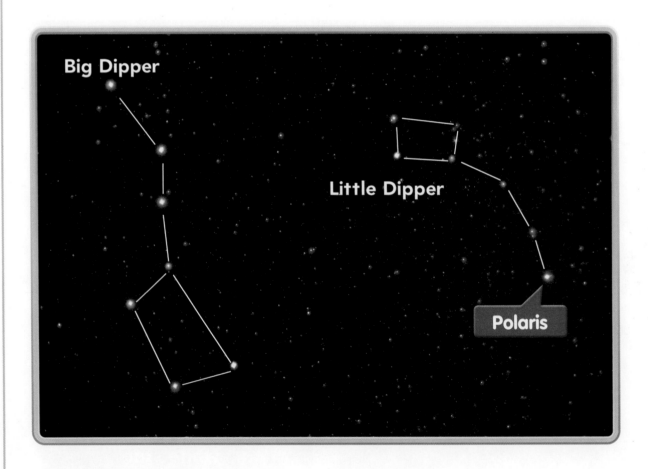

Big Dipper

Little Dipper

Polaris

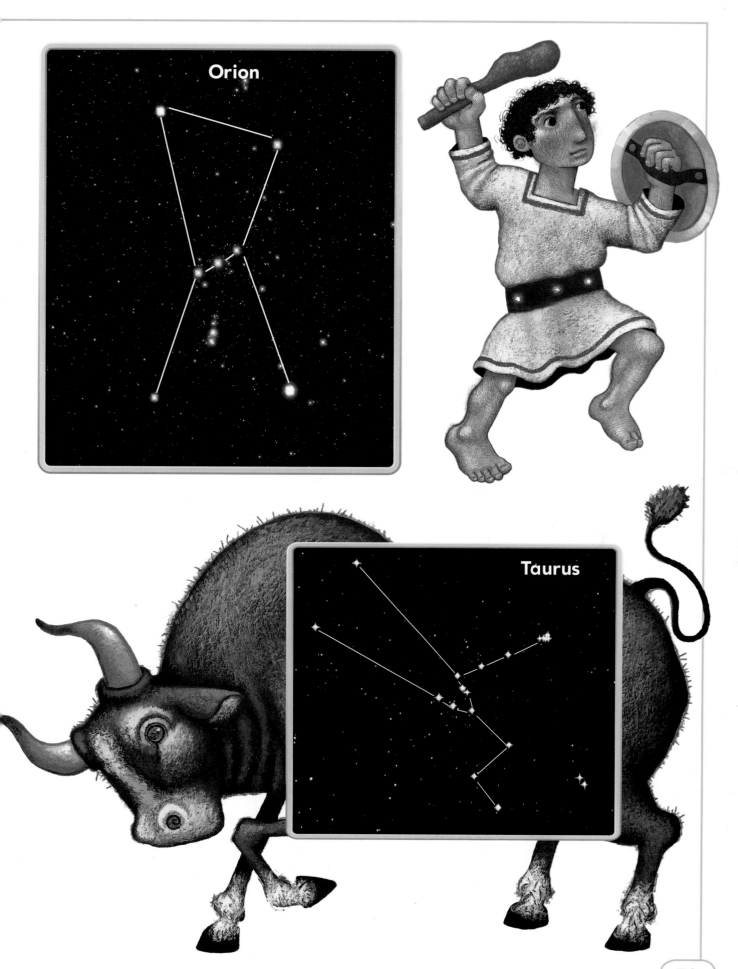

Orion

Taurus

79

Star Locations

Like the Moon, stars seem to move across the night sky. Earth is causing this motion. As Earth rotates, you see different parts of the night sky. You can see different stars in different seasons because Earth moves during the year.

Why does the Little Dipper seem to move?

Lesson Wrap-Up

❶ **Vocabulary** What is a **constellation**?

❷ **Reading Skill** How is the Sun different from other stars?

❸ **Compare** How are stars different from one another?

Technology Visit **www.eduplace.com/gascp** to find out more about stars.

Dr. Ellen Ochoa

Dr. Ellen Ochoa works for NASA. She is proud to have been the first Hispanic woman astronaut. She has visited space four times.

Dr. Ochoa likes to talk to children at schools. Her message is to work hard to reach your goals.

There is no gravity in space. Foot straps keep Dr. Ochoa from floating.

LINKS for Home and School

GPS STANDARDS S2E2d. Use observations and charts to record the shape of the moon for a period of time. **M2P5** Students will create and use pictures, manipulatives, models, and symbols to organize, record, and communicate mathematical ideas. **ELA2W1b.** Uses traditional organizational patterns for conveying information (e.g., chronological order, similarity and difference, answering questions).

Math Use a Calendar

This calendar shows the Moon phases for a month.

March						
Sun	Mon	Tue	Wed	Thu	Fri	Sat
					1	2
3	4	5	6	7	8	9
10	11	12	13	14	15	16
17	18	19	20	21	22	23
24	25	26	27	28	29	30
31						

1. How long does it take the Moon to go from new to full?

2. Draw a picture to show how the Moon will look on April 1.

 **Sky Flip Book**

Make a book with four cut pages like the one shown. Label the pages in the top half **Sun, Earth, Moon,** and **star.** Write about each sky object on the bottom half of the pages. Flip pages to match each word to its description.

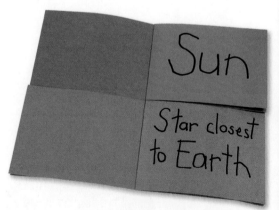

GeorgiaTask S2E2B

How does your shadow change?

- In the morning, stand outside in a sunny, open place.

- Have a partner trace your shoes and your shadow.

- Write down the time. Repeat this every two hours, always placing your feet in the same spot.

- How did your shadow change during the day?

Visual Summary

Movements of Earth and the Moon cause patterns.

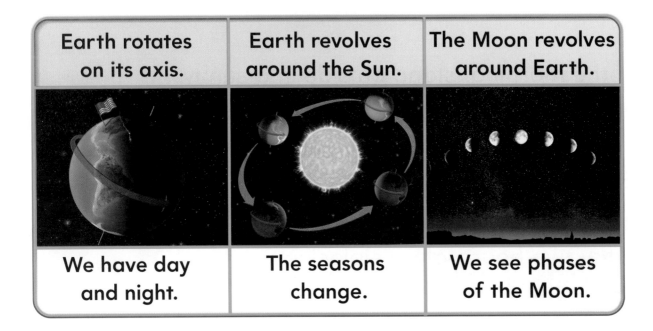

Earth rotates on its axis.	Earth revolves around the Sun.	The Moon revolves around Earth.
We have day and night.	The seasons change.	We see phases of the Moon.

Main Ideas

1. **What are some objects in the solar system?** `S2E1`
   (pp. 52–53)

2. **What causes night and day on Earth?** (p. 58) `S2E2`

3. **Why does the Moon appear to change?** (p. 70) `S2E2d`

4. **Why do some stars look brighter than others?** `S2E1a`
   (p. 77)

Vocabulary

Choose the correct word from the box.

5. A big ball of hot gases that gives off light

6. A large object that moves around the Sun

7. A large sphere made of rock

8. The path that one space object travels around another

S2CS7a

planet (p. 52)

orbit (p. 60)

Moon (p. 68)

star (p. 76)

Using Science Skills

9. **Use Models** How can using models of the Sun and the Moon help you understand the Moon's phases? **S2CS4b**

10. **Critical Thinking** How do shadows change? **S2E2b**

GPS CRCT Prep

Choose a word to complete the sentence.

11. The Sun is a

planet.
(A)

moon.
(B)

star.
(C)   **S2E1a**

GPS Test Practice

Choose the correct answer.

1. Some stars look bigger because they are

farther from Earth.	closer to Earth.	smaller.
Ⓐ	Ⓑ	Ⓒ

S2E1a

2. How will the shadow change when it is 12 o'clock noon?

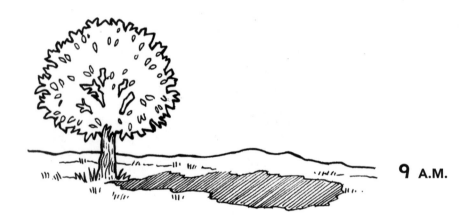

9 A.M.

It will be shorter.	It will not change.	It will be longer.
Ⓐ	Ⓑ	Ⓒ

S2E2b

3. There is a full Moon on June 30. What will the Moon look like 4 weeks later?

full Moon	first quarter Moon	new Moon
Ⓐ	Ⓑ	Ⓒ

S2E2d

4. What happens to the number of daylight hours in spring?

There are fewer.	There are more.	They stay the same.
Ⓐ	Ⓑ	Ⓒ

S2E2c

5. What caused these changes?

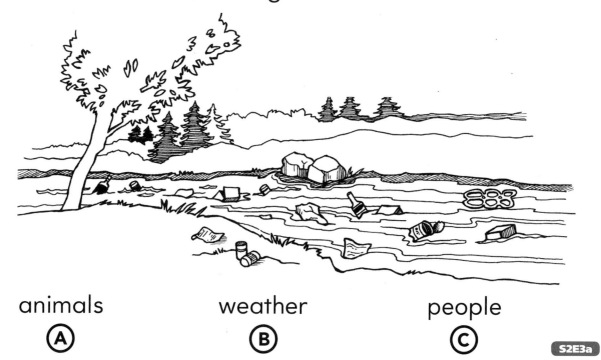

animals	weather	people
Ⓐ	Ⓑ	Ⓒ

S2E3a

GPS Checking Main Ideas

Write the correct answer.

6. Why does the Sun seem to change its position in the sky?

S2E2a

7. How can weather change the land?

S2E3a

 STANDARDS S2E1a. Describe the physical attributes of stars—size, brightness, and patterns.

You Can...

Discover More

Where are the stars during the day?

Stars are always in the sky. During the day, the Sun makes the sky too bright to see other stars. At night, the Sun does not shine on your part of Earth. Then you can see the light from other stars.

 Go to **www.eduplace.com/gascp** to find the stars during the day.

GEORGIA UNIT B SCIENCE

Physical Science

Cricket Connection

Visit www.eduplace.com/gascp to check out *Click, Ask,* and *Odyssey* magazine articles and activities.

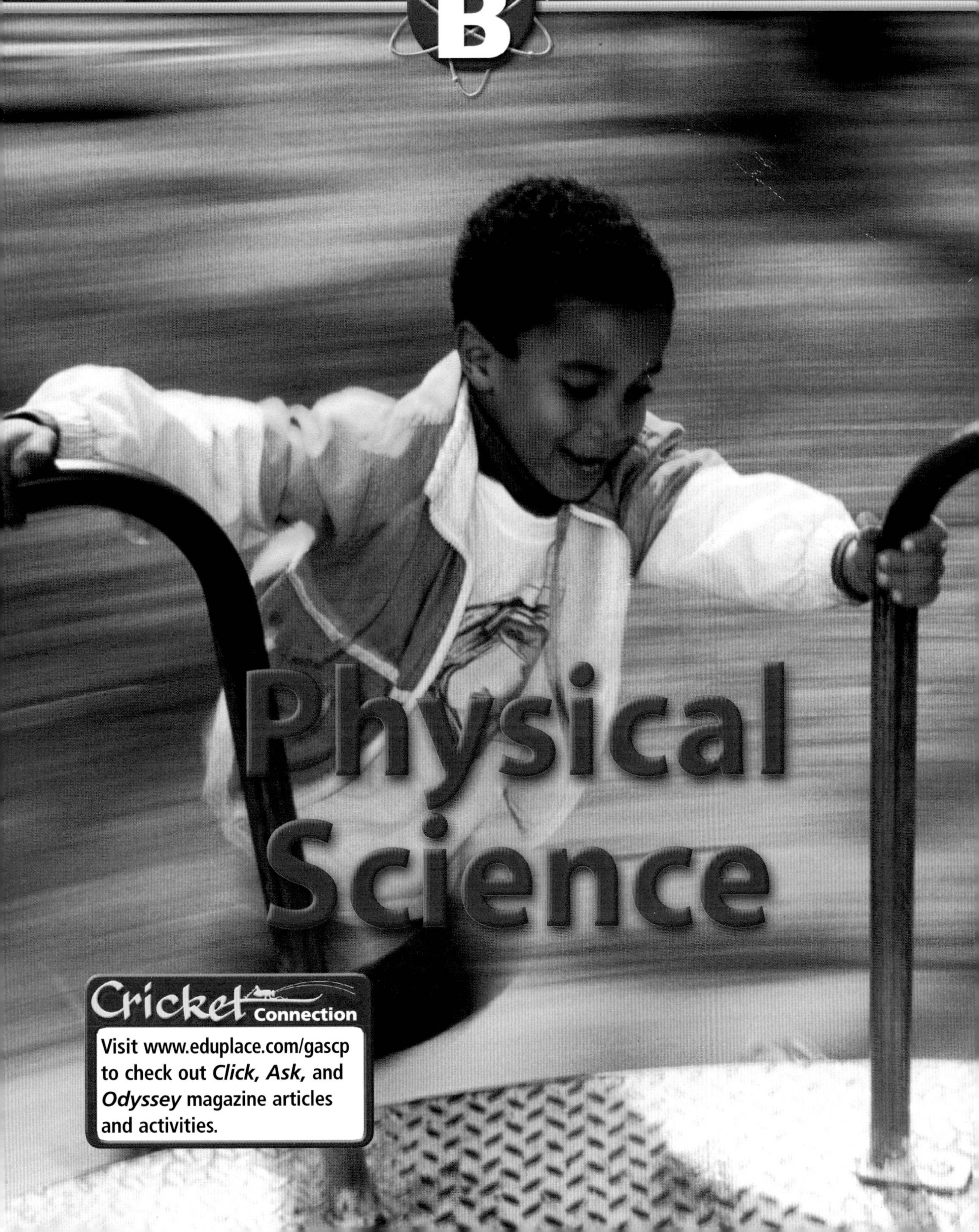

UNIT B

Physical Science

Reading in Science 90

Science in Georgia:
Physical Science Preview 92

Chapter 3
Comparing Matter 98

Chapter 4
Objects in Motion 132

Chapter 5
Heat and Light 166

Independent Reading

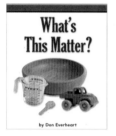

What's This
Matter?

It Must
Be Clay

Push or Pull

Georgia Fun Facts

A child sitting
on the outside of a
carousel goes faster than
a child sitting in the center.

Physical Science

The motion of objects can be observed and measured.

Start with a Poem

STANDARDS ELA2R4a. Reads a variety of texts for information and pleasure.

THE STEAM SHOVEL

by Rowena Bennett

The steam digger
Is much bigger
Than the biggest beast I know.
He snorts and roars
Like the dinosaurs
That lived long years ago.

He crouches low
On his tractor paws
And scoops the dirt up
With his jaws;
Then swings his long
Stiff neck around
And spits it out
Upon the ground.

Science in Georgia

How Does Speed Affect Motion?

Take a spin on this ride. As it speeds up, the swings moves faster. What happens when it slows down?

As the ride slows down, the swings move closer to the center of the ride.

Up and Down

Climbing uphill, the cars slowly reach the top of the track. Then, they zoom downhill. When does the speed on this ride change?

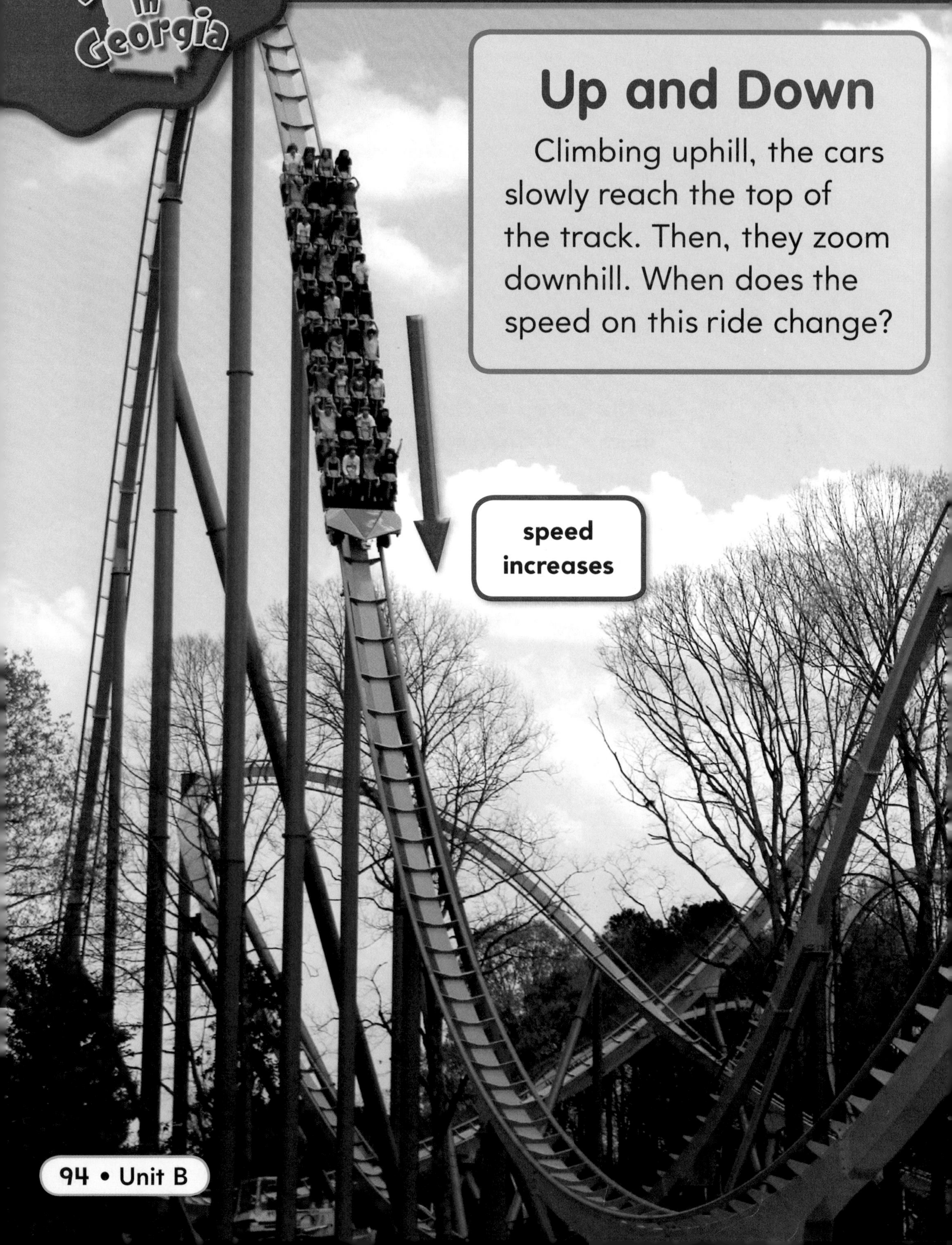

speed increases

speed decreases

Choose a word to complete the sentence.

1. As an object begins to move faster, it has _____ speed.

Ⓐ less

Ⓑ more

Ⓒ no

S2P3b

Performance Task

Move Objects

Find a box, a ball, a toy car, and a notebook. With a partner, take turns pushing each object forward. Then pull each object backward. Is it easier to push or to pull each object? Why are some objects easier to move than others?

GeorgiaTask S2P3B

Hands-On Project

GPS **STANDARDS S2CS3b.** Assemble, describe, take apart, and reassemble constructions using interlocking blocks, erector sets, and other things. **S2CS4a.** Identify the parts of things, such as toys or tools, and identify what things can do when put together that they could not do otherwise.

Math Relay Game

Make a game that uses pushes and pulls. You have to be fast and know your math to play this game!

What You Need
- 2 pencils
- 2 spools
- string
- paper clips
- 10 index cards

Step 1: Plan

- Form two teams.

- Make a clothesline using two spools, two pencils, and string.

- Have each team write a math problem on each card.

Step 2: Do It

- Have two children hold the ends of the clothesline.

- Team A puts one math problem on the clothesline with a paper clip.

- Team B pulls the clothesline and removes the card. They write the answer on the card and put it back on the clothesline.

- Team A pulls the clothesline back. They check the answer and put a new card on the clothesline.

- After all team A's problems have been solved, teams switch roles.

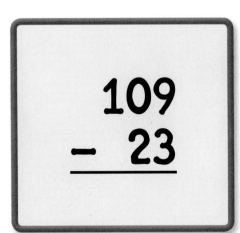

$$109 - 23$$

Step 3: Share

- How was pulling used in this game?

Chapter 3

Comparing Matter

Lesson Preview

LESSON 1

The desk, an apple, and a notebook are all solids. What solids are in your classroom?

LESSON 2

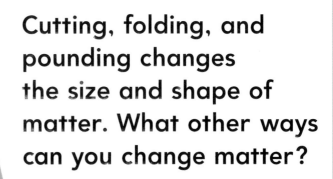

Cutting, folding, and pounding changes the size and shape of matter. What other ways can you change matter?

LESSON 3

Some tools can help you see. What might you see through a hand lens?

Vocabulary Preview

Vocabulary

properties p. 104

solid p. 106

liquid p. 106

gas p. 107

volume p. 108

mass p. 109

mixture p. 114

separate p. 114

dissolves p. 115

magnify p. 124

Picture Glossary p. H18

Vocabulary Skill

Find All the Meanings

volume

You might say, "Turn up the volume." Volume means to make louder or softer. Volume also means "the amount of space a liquid takes up."

liquid
A liquid is a state of matter that does not have its own shape.

properties

Color, shape, size, odor, and texture are properties.

mixture

A mixture is something made of two or more things.

separate

You can take apart, or separate, a mixture.

Georgia
Performance Standards

Start with Your Standards

Habits of Mind

S2CS2c. Give rough estimates of numerical answers to problems before doing them formally.

S2CS3a. Use ordinary hand tools and instruments to construct, measure, and look at objects.

Nature of Science

S2CS6b. Science involves collecting data and testing hypotheses.

Physical Science

S2P1a. Identify the three common states of matter as solid, liquid, or gas.

S2P1b. Investigate changes in objects by tearing, dissolving, melting, squeezing, etc.

GPS GEORGIA STANDARDS

S2CS2c. Give rough estimates of numerical answers to problems before doing them formally.

S2P1a. Identify the three common states of matter as solid, liquid, or gas.

? Essential Question: How Can You Compare Matter?

Science and You

Knowing about matter can help you describe things.

Inquiry Skill

Measure You can use tools to measure length, volume, and mass.

What You Need

balance

gram cubes

golf ball

measuring cup and water

STEP 1

Measure Matter

Steps

1. Hold a golf ball in one hand. Estimate how many gram cubes it equals.

2. **Measure** Use a balance to check your estimate.

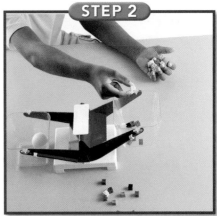

STEP 2

3. **Measure** Pour water into a measuring cup to the 100-milliliter mark.

4. **Measure** Put a golf ball into the measuring cup. Measure the change in the water level.

STEP 3

Think and Share

1. **Compare** How did your measurement of the ball compare to your estimate?

2. How did the number of milliliters in the cup change when you added the ball?

Guided Inquiry

Work Together Find other objects that can be measured on a balance. Talk about how to sort them by their measurements.

Habits of Mind

Vocabulary

properties

solid

liquid

gas

volume

mass

▶ **Reading Skill**

Categorize and Classify

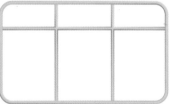

GPS **S2P1a.** Identify the three common states of matter as solid, liquid, or gas.

Describing Objects

You can describe objects by their properties. Color, shape, size, odor, and texture are **properties**. A balloon can be red or yellow. A slipper can be soft and fuzzy. A penny is round and flat.

You can describe objects by the materials from which they are made. A penny is made of copper. Marbles are made of glass. A spring toy can be made of plastic.

Other properties tell what objects or materials do. Some objects can bend without breaking. Others cannot. Some will stretch. Others will tear apart. Some materials will let light pass through. Others will not. A marble will roll. A rock will sink in water. A pencil will float.

▶ **Classify** What are properties that you can see?

Which objects will let light pass through? Which will not?

Express Lab

Activity Card 8
Classify Properties

States of Matter

All things are made of matter. The three states of matter are solid, liquid, and gas.

A **solid** is a state of matter that has its own size and shape. A toy boat is a solid. If you toss it into a pool, it will keep its size and shape.

A **liquid** is a state of matter that does not have its own shape. Water is a liquid. Liquids flow and take the shape of a container.

What are the solids, the liquids, and the gases in the picture?

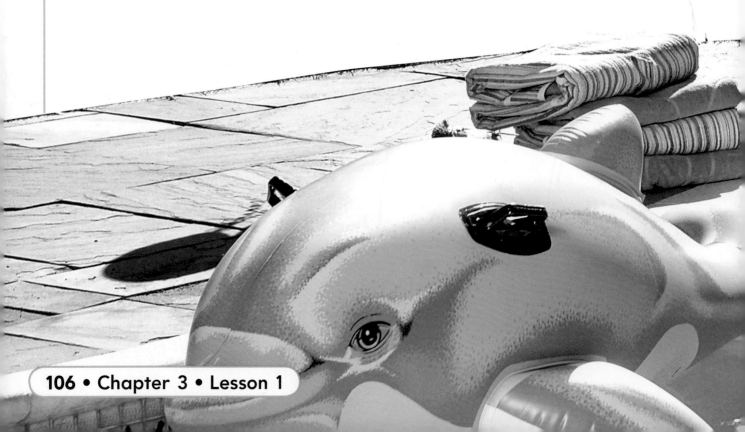

A balloon holds a gas.

A **gas** is a state of matter that spreads out to fill a space. It has no shape of its own. A gas always fills a closed container and comes out when you open the container.

▶ **Classify** Is juice a solid, a liquid, or a gas?

solid

liquid

Using Tools to Measure

All matter takes up space. The amount of space that matter takes up can be measured. You can measure the length, width, and height of a solid object with a ruler. You can measure the amount of space that a liquid takes up, or **volume**, with a measuring cup.

You pour a liquid into a measuring cup to find its volume.

Mass is the amount of matter in an object. All matter has mass. You can measure the mass of an object with a balance. The object sits on one side of the balance. Then you add mass units until the sides are even.

▶ **Classify** Name two properties that can be measured.

Lesson Wrap-Up

❶ **Vocabulary** What are color, size, shape, and texture?

❷ **Reading Skill** Look at the picture. Name a solid. Name a liquid. Name a gas.

❸ **Measure** What tool would you use to measure volume?

💻 **Technology** Visit **www.eduplace.com/gascp** to find out more about comparing matter.

Sand to Glass

What can you do with sand?
If you have enough heat, you can change sand into glass!

Glassmakers put sand into a *very* hot oven. The heat melts the sand and changes it into a liquid. The sand turns into a stretchy goo. The goo can then be shaped. As the goo cools, it hardens and turns into a solid, smooth glass!

Most glass begins as sand just like the kind you find at beaches.

Dale Chihuly is a glass artist. He made these colorful glass balls. He begins with pure white sand and then adds colors when the sand melts.

GPS **GEORGIA STANDARDS**

S2CS6b. Science involves collecting data and testing hypotheses.
S2P1b. Investigate changes in objects by tearing, dissolving, melting, squeezing, etc.

? How Does Matter Change?

Essential Question

Science and You

When glue hardens, it changes from a liquid to a solid.

Inquiry Skill

Compare Tell how objects are alike or different.

What You Need

foil

butter

wooden block

lamp

Compare Matter

Steps

1. Make two trays from foil.

2. Put some butter on one tray. Put a block on the other tray.

3. **Predict** Put the trays under a lamp. Tell what you think will happen after 10 minutes. Then observe. **Safety:** The lamp is hot!

4. **Compare** How did your prediction compare to your results?

Think and Share

1. **Compare** Tell how the changes to the butter and the block were alike and different.

2. **Infer** What do you think caused the changes?

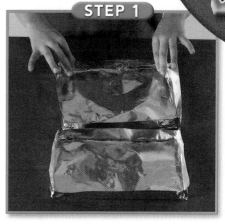

STEP 1

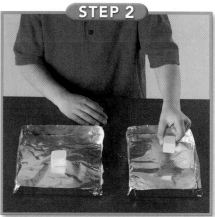

STEP 2

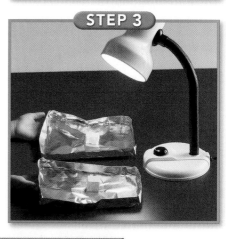

STEP 3

Habits of Mind

Guided Inquiry

Experiment Repeat the activity with other solids. You might use an ice cube and a book. What can you infer about solids?

▶ **Vocabulary**

mixture

separate

dissolves

⏵ **Reading Skill**

Draw Conclusions

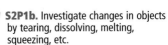

GPS **S2P1b.** Investigate changes in objects by tearing, dissolving, melting, squeezing, etc.

Mixing Matter

You can put matter together to make a mixture. A **mixture** is something made of two or more things.

When you make a mixture, there is no new matter. Each part is still there. You can take apart, or **separate**, a mixture.

Trail mix is a mixture that is easy to separate.

Trail Mix

2 cups cereal
1 cup raisins
1 cup peanuts
1 cup dry fruit

Some mixtures are easy to separate. The parts stay the same size and shape. They are easy to see.

Some mixtures are hard to separate. When you stir drink mix powder into water, it **dissolves**, or mixes completely with water. The powder breaks up into pieces too small to see. But it is still powder.

▶ **Draw Conclusions** Why are some mixtures harder to separate than others?

What is happening to the powder?

Express Lab

Activity Card 9
Time a Change of State

cutting paper

sanding wood

Changing Matter

You can change the properties of solid matter in many ways. You can change the shape of matter by cutting it. You can change the size or shape of matter by breaking it into smaller pieces. You can tear paper into different sizes and shapes.

You can sift sand to separate the different-sized pieces. You can pound a lump of clay until it is flat. You can sand the edges of a block of wood to make them smooth. These kinds of changes do not change the material that the matter is made of.

pounding clay

▶ **Draw Conclusions** How are you changing matter when you pound clay?

Changing States

Matter can change from one state to another. Taking away heat causes some liquids to change to solids. Adding heat causes some solids to change to liquids.

An ice cube is solid water. When ice is heated, it changes to liquid water. If the water is heated, it can evaporate and change to a gas, or water vapor.

How did the juice change from the pitcher to the plate?

All matter does not change the same way when heated. Some things melt quickly. Some things melt slowly. Other things do not melt at all.

▶ **Draw Conclusions** If a solid changes to a liquid, what can you say happened?

Butter melts quickly.

Lesson Wrap-Up

❶ **Vocabulary** What is a **mixture**?

❷ **Reading Skill** What causes matter to change state?

❸ **Compare** How are butter and jelly alike and different?

Technology Visit www.eduplace.com/gascp to find out more about how matter changes.

Changing Matter to Make Coins

Coins are made by changing matter. It takes many steps to turn raw metal into a coin.

1

A quarter is made from two metals. The two metals begin as solids.

2

The metals are heated and change to liquids. The liquids are mixed together.

3

The mixture is cooled and becomes solid again. It is rolled out into sheets.

GPS **STANDARDS** S2P1a. Identify the three common states of matter as solid, liquid, or gas.

SOCIAL STUDIES **LINK**

A new state quarter is made every 10 weeks. Five different state quarters have been made each year since 1999.

4

A machine cuts the metal into blank circles.

5

The pictures and words are pressed onto the coins.

Sharing Ideas

1. **Write About It** Name the ways that matter is changed to make a quarter.

2. **Talk About It** How might the quarter change after it is made?

Lesson 3

GEORGIA STANDARDS

S2CS3a. Use ordinary hand tools and instruments to construct, measure, and look at objects.
S2P1 Students will investigate the properties of matter and changes that occur in objects.

Essential Question

How Does Matter Look Up Close?

Science and You

A hand lens can help you learn more about the world around you.

Inquiry Skill

Observe You can use tools and your senses to find out about something.

What You Need

objects

hand lens

Observe Objects

Steps

STEP 1

1. **Observe** Choose an object to observe. Write or draw what you see.

STEP 2

2. **Observe** Look at the same object with a hand lens. Write or draw what you see.

3. **Communicate** Show your drawings to a partner. Talk about what you saw.

STEP 3

4. Choose another object. Repeat the activity.

Think and Share

1. What does the hand lens do?

2. **Compare** How is what you see with the hand lens different from what you see without the hand lens?

Guided Inquiry

Be an Inventor A hand lens can make a task easier. Think of a task that you do at home or at school. Invent a way to use a hand lens to make the job easier.

Vocabulary

magnify

▶ **Reading Skill**

Main Idea and Details

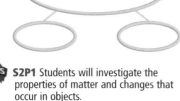

GPS **S2P1** Students will investigate the properties of matter and changes that occur in objects.

Tools that Magnify

Matter is made of parts too small to see with only your eyes. When you look at a leaf, you see a green shape with lines in it. But the leaf might have colors that you cannot see. It might have smaller lines all over it. To see these parts, you can use a tool.

Some tools can make objects look larger, or **magnify** them. You may have used a hand lens to magnify objects. Sometimes scientists use a microscope to magnify objects even more.

▶ **Main Idea** Why are tools needed to see small parts of matter?

Ants look like this without a magnifying tool.

Express Lab

Activity Card 10
Observe Details

An ant looks like this
through a hand lens. ▶

◀ An ant looks like this
through a microscope.

Matter Up Close

When you use a tool to magnify, you can see the small parts of matter. The pictures show how things look when magnified.

granite feather fish scales

sugar cube sesame seed roll strawberry

Lesson Wrap-Up

❶ **Vocabulary** If you **magnify** something, what do you do?

❷ **Reading Skill** What two tools can help you see small parts of things?

❸ **Observe** What might you see if you used a hand lens to look at an ant?

Technology Visit **www.eduplace.com/gascp** to find out more about tools that magnify.

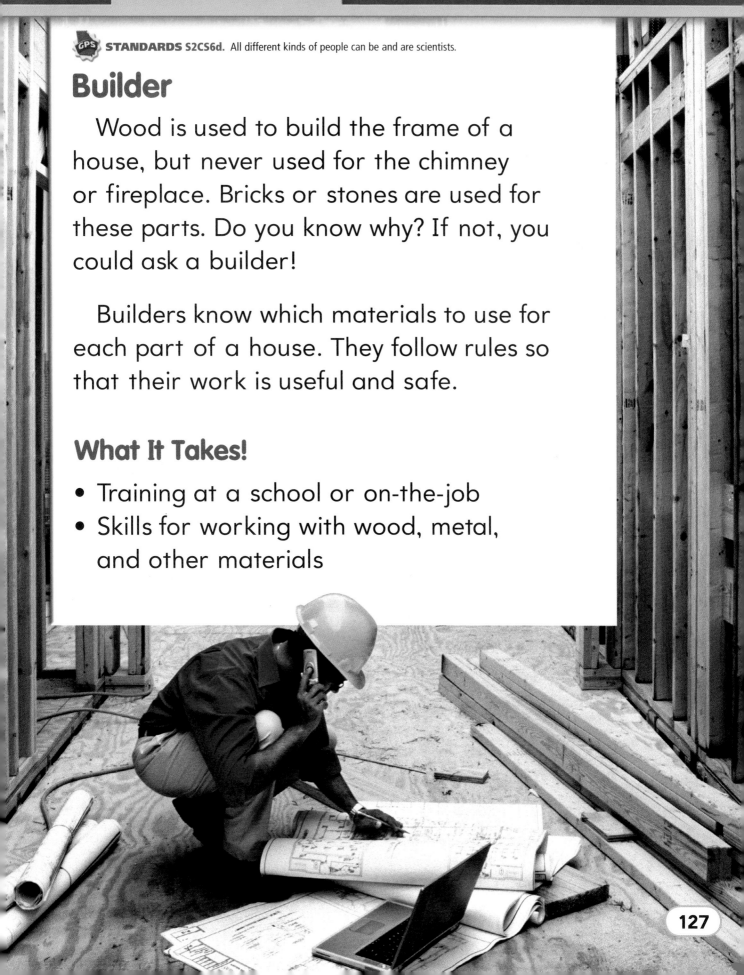

Careers in Science

GPS STANDARDS S2CS6d. All different kinds of people can be and are scientists.

Builder

Wood is used to build the frame of a house, but never used for the chimney or fireplace. Bricks or stones are used for these parts. Do you know why? If not, you could ask a builder!

Builders know which materials to use for each part of a house. They follow rules so that their work is useful and safe.

What It Takes!

- Training at a school or on-the-job
- Skills for working with wood, metal, and other materials

127

LINKS
for Home and School

STANDARDS S2CS2d. Make quantitative estimates of familiar lengths, weights, and time intervals, and check them by measuring. **M2D1a.** Organize and display data using picture graphs, Venn diagrams, bar graphs, and simple charts/tables to record results. **ELA2W1a.** Writes text of a length appropriate to address a topic and tell the story.

Math Measure Length

Choose three objects to measure. Estimate how long you think each is. Then use a ruler to measure each object. Record the measurements in a chart like the one shown. Compare the measurements.

Lengths of Objects		
Object	Estimate	Measure

 **Describe Matter**

List words to describe a solid, a liquid, or a gas. Share your list with a partner. Then add other words to your list that describe matter. Write a poem using your list.

Water
liquid
clear

GeorgiaTask S2P1A

How are mixtures different?

- Pour warm water into a cup and stir in a spoonful of sand. Observe and record what happens to the mixture.

- In another cup of warm water, add salt and stir. Observe and record what happens.

- How are the mixtures different? What happened to the salt? What happened to the sand?

Visual Summary

Matter is classified by its properties.

A solid has its own size and shape.	A liquid does not have its own shape.	A gas spreads out to fill a space.

Main Ideas

1. What is a solid? (p. 106) `S2P1a`

2. How are gases and liquids alike? (pp. 106–107) `S2P1a`

3. What happens to some solids when they are heated? (p. 118) `S2P1b`

4. Why would you use a magnifying tool? (p. 124) `S2CS3a`

Vocabulary

Choose the correct word from the box.

5. The amount of matter in an object

6. To take apart

7. Mixes completely with water

8. Color, size, shape, odor, and texture

properties (p. 104)

mass (p. 109)

separate (p. 114)

dissolves (p. 115)

Using Science Skills

9. **Measure** What tools can you use to measure matter? Tell how.
   S2CS3a

10. **Critical Thinking** What changes to matter happen in nature, without help from people?
    S2P1b

CRCT Prep

Choose a word to complete the sentence.

11. Mixing completely with water is to

   dissolve.   separate.   magnify.
     Ⓐ   Ⓑ   Ⓒ   S2P1b

Chapter 4

Objects in Motion

LESSON 1

A ball can bounce up and down. What other ways can a ball move?

LESSON 2

People use a cart to carry things. How do they make it move?

LESSON 3

These boys will run a race. As they race, how will you know who is faster?

Vocabulary Preview

Vocabulary

position p. 138

motion p. 140

gravity p. 141

force p. 146

friction p. 148

simple machine p. 158

ramp p. 158

lever p. 159

pulley p. 160

Picture Glossary p. H18

Vocabulary Skill

Use Pictures

motion

Look at the picture of motion. A picture helps you know the meaning of a word. What do you know about motion from this picture?

force

A force is a push or a pull.

ramp

A ramp is a slanted tool used to move things from one level to another.

lever

A lever is a bar that moves around a fixed point.

motion

An object that is in motion changes its position, or moves from one place to another.

Start with Your Standards

Habits of Mind

S2CS3c. Make something that can actually be used to perform a task, using paper, cardboard, wood, plastic, metal, or existing objects.

S2CS5a. Describe and compare things in terms of number, shape, texture, size, weight, color, and motion.

Nature of Science

S2CS6c. Scientists often repeat experiments multiple times and subject their ideas to criticism by other scientists who may disagree with them and do further tests.

Physical Science

S2P3a. Demonstrate how pushing and pulling an object affects the motion of the object.

S2P3b. Demonstrate the effects of changes of speed on an object.

Lesson 1

GEORGIA STANDARDS

S2CS5a. Describe and compare things in terms of number, shape, texture, size, weight, color, and motion.
S2P3a. Demonstrate how pushing and pulling an object affects the motion of the object.

How Do Things Move?

Essential Question

Science and You

Knowing how things move can help you describe them.

Inquiry Skill

Ask Questions When you ask questions about what you observe, you can learn more.

What You Need

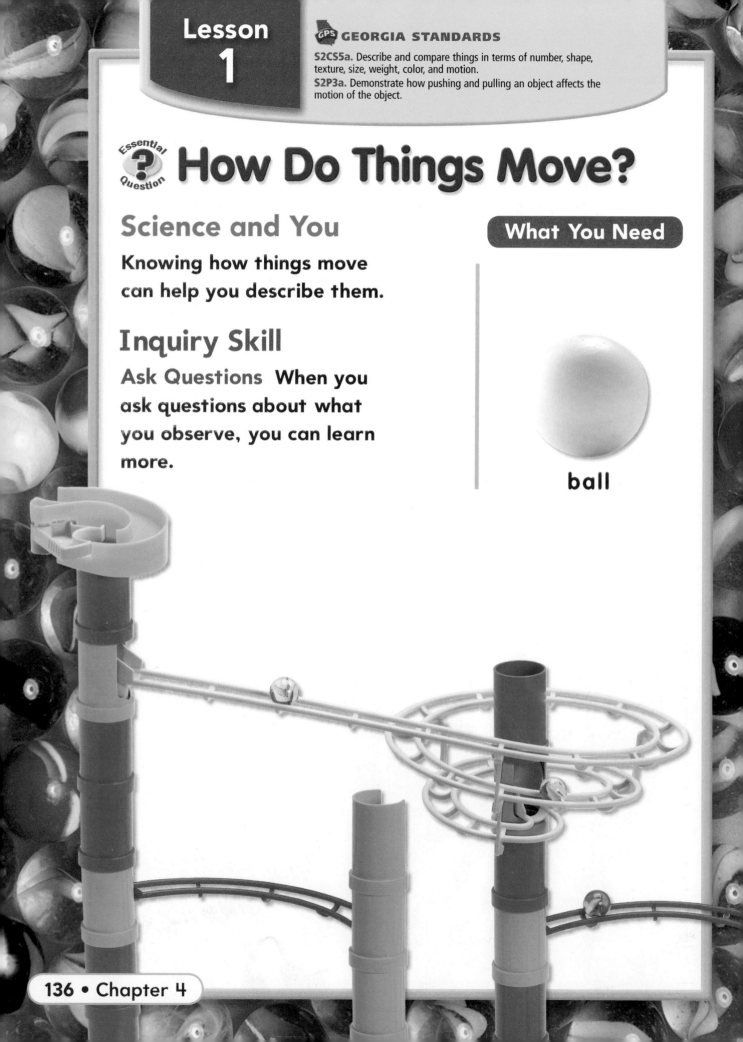

ball

Observe Motion

Steps

1. **Observe** Sit on the floor across from a classmate. See how many ways you can make the ball move across the floor.

2. **Record Data** Use a chart like the one shown. List the different ways that the ball moved. Write what you did to cause each motion.

3. **Observe** Roll the ball across a desk or table. Observe and record what happens.

STEP 1

STEP 2

How the Ball Moved	What I Did

STEP 3

Think and Share

1. What did you do to make the ball move in different ways?

2. What happened when the ball reached the edge of the desk or table? Tell why.

Guided Inquiry

Ask Questions What else can you do to make the ball move? Finish the question. What would happen if I _____?

Vocabulary

position

motion

gravity

▶ **Reading Skill**

Draw Conclusions

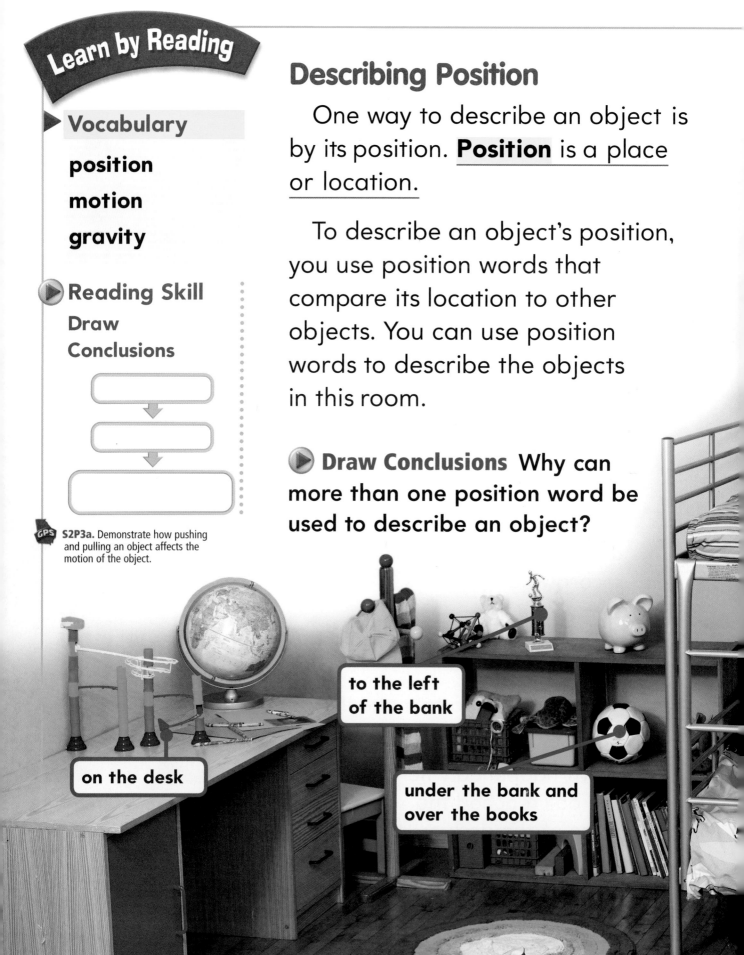

GPS **S2P3a.** Demonstrate how pushing and pulling an object affects the motion of the object.

Describing Position

One way to describe an object is by its position. **Position** is a place or location.

To describe an object's position, you use position words that compare its location to other objects. You can use position words to describe the objects in this room.

▶ **Draw Conclusions** Why can more than one position word be used to describe an object?

to the left of the bank

on the desk

under the bank and over the books

above the bed

on top of the bed

next to the bed

139

Changing Position

An object that is in **motion** changes its position, or moves from one place to another. One way to tell if an object is moving is to compare its position to objects around it. There are different kinds of motion. An object can move in a straight line, back and forth, or even in a circle.

◀ back and forth

▼ in a circle

Express Lab

Activity Card 11
Describe an Object's
Location

▼ How will this ball move next?

◄ in a straight line

An object can also move up and down. Objects drop to the ground unless something holds them up. This change in position is caused by gravity. **Gravity** is a force that pulls all objects toward each other.

▶ **Draw Conclusions** Does a baseball move in a straight line or a circle when hit?

Lesson Wrap-Up

1. **Vocabulary** How do you describe the **position** of an object?

2. **Reading Skill** Why is the ground beneath a tree often covered with leaves in fall?

3. **Ask Questions** What else do you want to know about how things move?

Technology Visit **www.eduplace.com/gascp** to find out more about motion.

STANDARDS S2P3b. Demonstrate the effects of changes of speed on an object.

Fast, Faster, Fastest!

How would you like to ride in a car that is faster than many jet airplanes? Meet the Thrust SSC, the fastest car in the world!

The Thrust SSC uses two jet engines for power. In 1997, it set a world record by reaching the amazing speed of 763 miles per hour!

The Thrust SSC can travel the distance of three football fields in less than a second!

The world record was set on a dry salt lake in Black Rock Desert, Nevada.

Lesson 2

GEORGIA STANDARDS

S2CS3c. Make something that can actually be used to perform a task, using paper, cardboard, wood, plastic, metal, or existing objects.
S2P3a. Demonstrate how pushing and pulling an object affects the motion of the object.

What Do Forces Do?

Science and You

Knowing about forces can help you know how to move something.

Inquiry Skill

Compare Tell how objects or events are alike and different.

What You Need

goggles

chair

cart, rubber band, tape, and ruler

classroom objects

Make Things Move

Steps

STEP 1

1. **Measure** Place two strips of tape 15 centimeters apart. Put a chair leg next to one strip of tape. Put a rubber band around the chair leg. Stretch the rubber band. **Safety:** Wear goggles!

STEP 2

2. **Observe** Place a cart against the band. Pull the cart back to the second line. Let it go. Use tape to mark where the cart stops.

STEP 3

3. **Compare** Put an object on the cart. Repeat step 2. Compare the distances.

Think and Share

1. Why do you think the cart went different distances?

2. **Predict** How could you make the heavier cart go the same distance as the lighter cart?

Guided Inquiry

Work together With a partner find different objects and toys that have moveable parts. Then name the parts that help them to move.

Vocabulary

force

friction

Reading Skill

Cause and Effect

S2P3a. Demonstrate how pushing and pulling an object affects the motion of the object.

Forces and Motion

To move an object, you use force. A **force** is a push or a pull. A large force is needed to move a heavy object. A smaller force can move lighter objects.

When you push or pull an object, you give the object energy. The amount of energy depends on the size of the force.

▼ large push

▼ small push

Which kick will make the ball move farther?

▼ pull

A large force gives an object more energy. If you kick a ball with a lot of force, the ball moves fast and goes far. If you kick the same ball with less force, the ball moves more slowly for a shorter distance.

▶ **Cause and Effect** If you kick a ball with a little force, what will happen?

Express Lab

Activity Card 12
Observe a Ball's Motion

Friction and Motion

Friction is a force that makes an object slow down when it rubs against another object. When the tires on your bike rub against the road, the rubbing causes friction. Riding on a rough surface causes more friction than riding on a smooth surface. You have to pedal harder when there is more friction.

Friction between the brakes and the wheel stops the bike.

cement

grass

gravel

← less friction   more friction →

Changing Direction

Forces can change the direction of a moving object. When you bounce a ball, you push it with your hand. It keeps moving down until it hits the ground. Then it changes direction and bounces back up. You push the ball again. The direction of the ball keeps changing.

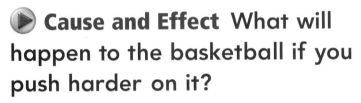 **Cause and Effect** What will happen to the basketball if you push harder on it?

Lesson Wrap-Up

❶ **Vocabulary** What is a **force**?

❷ **Reading Skill** What happens when a bicycle moves from a smooth surface to a rough surface?

❸ **Compare** Is it easier to lift a backpack filled with books or an empty backpack? Tell why.

💻 **Technology** Visit **www.eduplace.com/gascp** to find out more about forces.

Safety in Motion

How can science help you stay safe?
Let the Safety Team tell you all about it!

Cast
Narrator
Joan
Miguel
Sue
Leon

STANDARDS S2P3a. Demonstrate how pushing and pulling an object affects the motion of the object.

READING LINK

Narrator: The Safety Team uses what they know about science to stay safe while they have fun. Listen to what they have to say.

Joan: When I roller skate, I am in motion. I wear a helmet to protect my head. If I fall, the helmet will hit the ground before my head does and take in most of the force.

Miguel: Don't forget knee pads, elbow pads, and wrist guards. If you fall, your knees, elbows, wrists, and hands will be protected, too.

Narrator: The Safety Team thinks about science and safety on the playground, too.

Miguel: Playground swings move back and forth. I never walk in front of, or behind, a moving swing. If I did, I could get knocked over!

Joan: A push is a force. When you push someone, even for fun, the person will move. Gravity might pull the person to the ground. That can really hurt! I find it is best to follow the No Pushing rule.

Narrator: Understanding science can help keep you safe at home.

Leon: I like to play with toys that have wheels. I push or pull them in different directions, both indoors and outdoors.

Sue: Me too! And wheels move fastest on a smooth surface because there is less friction.

Leon: But, if a toy with wheels is left out, someone might step on it. The toy's wheels could make it move, and the person could fall and get hurt.

Sue: So, remember to put away wheeled toys after playing with them.

Narrator: Science and safety matter in the car too. In fact, they can save your life!

Sue: I always wear a safety belt. A moving car might stop suddenly or hit something. That force can make you move inside the car. A safety belt helps keep you in your seat. It can stop you from banging into a window or other things in the car.

Narrator: Time is up. We have to put on the brakes. We hope you will be part of the Safety Team.

All: And use science to stay safe!

Sharing Ideas

1. **Write About It** Tell about a time when you should have been more careful and why.

2. **Talk About It** Share ideas about things you do at home to keep you and your family members safe.

GEORGIA STANDARDS

S2CS6c. Scientists often repeat experiments multiple times and subject their ideas to criticism by other scientists who may disagree with them and do further tests.
S2P3b. Demonstrate the effects of changes of speed on an object.

Essential Question

What Can You Do with Motion?

Science and You

You can move things more easily when you know about simple machines.

Inquiry Skill

Measure Use tools to find out how far and how much time.

What You Need

masking tape

2 toy cars

meter stick

stopwatch

STEP 1

Measure Motion

Steps

① Mark a start line on the floor with tape. Put one toy car on the start line.

② **Measure** Push the car forward. Measure the time from when it starts to when it stops.

STEP 2

③ **Measure** Use a meter stick to see how far the car moved.

④ Repeat steps 1–3 with the other car. Use the same force. Compare the results.

STEP 3

Think and Share

1. **Use Data** Which car went farther? Which car took more time?

2. **Infer** What can you infer about going a longer distance?

Guided Inquiry

Experiment Plan ways to make the car move farther. Test your ideas. Tell which idea worked the best. Tell why you think so.

Habits of Mind

Vocabulary

simple machine

ramp

lever

pulley

Reading Skill
Compare and Contrast

GPS **S2P3b.** Demonstrate the effects of changes of speed on an object.

It takes more time to go a longer distance.

Measuring Motion

Motion can be measured in different ways. You can measure how far something travels. A swimmer may travel a distance of 50 meters or 100 meters.

You also can measure the time it takes to go a certain distance. In a swimming race, a stopwatch is used to find the time it takes each swimmer to go a certain distance.

Fastest Swimming Times

Distance	Time
50 meters	about 22 seconds
100 meters	about 48 seconds
200 meters	about 1 minute, 44 seconds
400 meters	about 3 minutes, 40 seconds

The swimmer who finishes first moves at a faster speed than the others. The rate at which that swimmer is kicking may be faster than the rates of others. Moving at a faster rate usually means that it will take less time to go a certain distance.

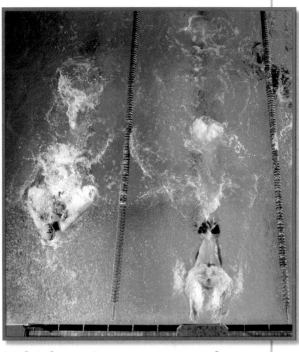

Which swimmer moved faster?

▶ **Compare and Contrast**
What is the difference between a fast swimmer and a slow swimmer?

Express Lab

Activity Card 13
Measure Motion

Using Ramps

A **simple machine** is a tool that can make it easier to move objects. A **ramp** is a slanted tool used to move things from one level to another. Movers must move heavy objects from the ground into a truck. It takes less force to move things up a ramp than to lift them straight up off the ground.

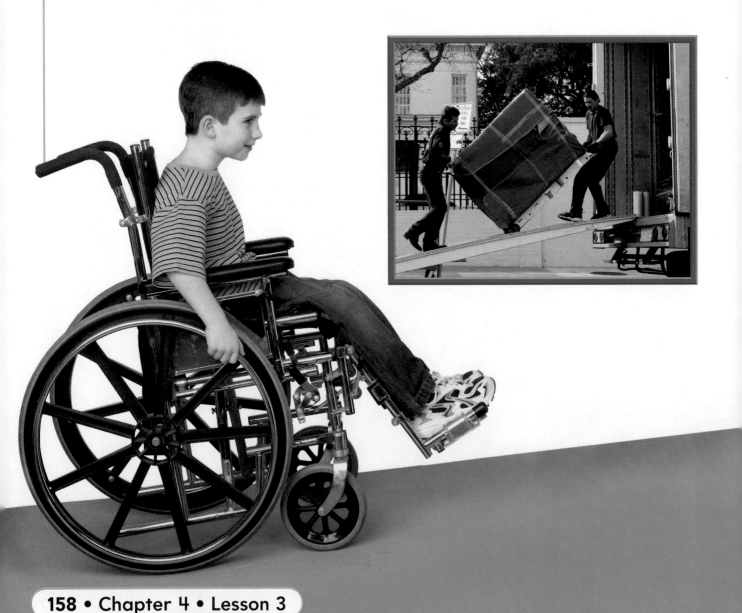

Using Levers

A **lever** is a bar that moves around a fixed point. A lever can change the direction of a motion. Different kinds of levers are used for different jobs.

▲ When you lift one end of a can opener, the other end pushes down on the can.

▶ **Compare and Contrast** How are a ramp and a lever alike?

A heavier object on one side of a balance will lift the lighter object on the other side. ▼

▲ You push down on one end of a screwdriver and the other end lifts off the lid.

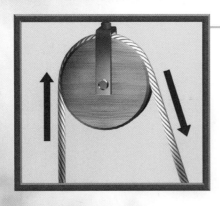

pulley

Using Pulleys

Another machine used to lift objects is a pulley. A **pulley** is a wheel with a groove through which a rope or chain moves. When you raise a flag, you pull down on the rope on one side of the pulley. The rope on the other side goes up. A pulley changes the direction of a force.

Lesson Wrap-Up

❶ **Vocabulary** What is a bar that moves around a fixed point?

❷ **Reading Skill** How are all simple machines alike?

❸ **Measure** How can you measure the distance that a ball rolls?

Technology Visit www.eduplace.com/gascp to find out more about simple machines.

STANDARDS S2CS6d. All different kinds of people can be and are scientists.

Animator

An animator makes cartoon characters seem to come to life. Animators must understand position and motion.

An animator draws pictures or makes models. Each one is just a little different from the last. Filming the pictures or models one after another makes them seem to move.

What It Takes!

- Talent in art and design
- Good math skills

LINKS
for Home and School

 STANDARDS S2CS2c. Give rough estimates of numerical answers to problems before doing them formally. **M2M1b.** Estimate lengths, and then measure to determine if estimations were reasonable. **ELA2W1a.** Writes text of length appropriate to address a topic and tell the story.

Math Measure Distances

Estimate the distance from your desk to the board. Record your estimate in a chart like the one shown. Then use a measuring tool to find the actual distance. Repeat for two other distances. Compare the measurements.

Classroom Distances			
Starting Point	Ending Point	Estimated Distance	Actual Distance
desk	board		

 ## Moving Ball

Football, soccer, and tennis are some sports that use balls. Write about a sport that uses a ball. Tell how that ball might move. Describe how force changes the speed of the ball.

GeorgiaTask S2P2A

How do objects move differently?

- Push and pull different objects.

- Use a ruler to measure the distance each object moved.

- Sort the list into objects that kept moving after you stopped pushing them.

- Sort the list by the distance each object traveled.

- Why did different objects continue to move or not move?

Visual Summary

Forces cause objects to move.

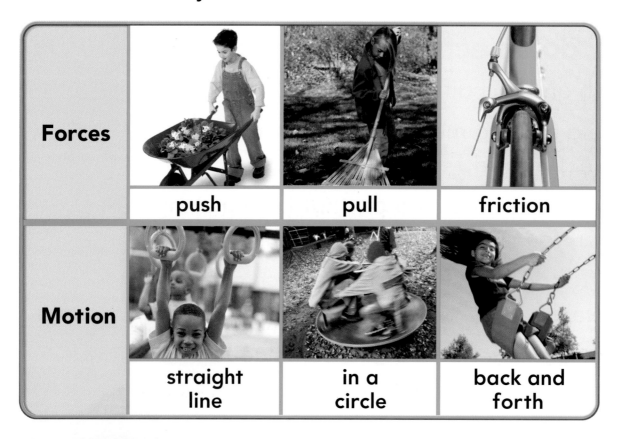

Forces	push	pull	friction
Motion	straight line	in a circle	back and forth

Main Ideas

1. How will an object move when pushed with a small force? (p. 147) `S2P3a`

2. How can gravity make something move? (p. 141) `S2P3a`

3. How will an object move when a large force is used? (p. 147) `S2P3b`

4. What is a tool that makes it easier to move objects? (pp. 158–159) `S2CS3a`

Vocabulary

Choose the correct word from the box.

S2CS7a

5. A push or a pull

6. A wheel with a groove through which a rope or chain moves

7. A slanted tool used to move things from one level to another

8. Movement from one place to another

motion (p. 140)
force (p. 146)
ramp (p. 158)
pulley (p. 160)

Using Science Skills

9. **Compare** Is more force needed to move a heavy object or a lighter object? S2P3a

10. **Critical Thinking** What happens when an object changes speed? S2P3b

GPS CRCT Prep

Choose a word to complete the sentence.

11. A _____ force will make an object move faster.

slower
Ⓐ

greater
Ⓑ

smaller
Ⓒ

S2P3b

Chapter 5

Heat
and Light

Cumberland Island, GA

Lesson Preview

LESSON 1

On a cold night, a fire keeps you warm. What are some other ways you use heat?

LESSON 2

Light from this lamp helps you see. What other sources of light can you think of?

Vocabulary

heat p. 172

melt p. 175

light p. 180

Picture Glossary p. H18

Vocabulary Skill

Use Pictures

light

Say the word aloud. Look at the picture for this word. Use clues from the picture to help you understand what the word means.

heat
Heat is a kind of energy that makes things warm.

melt
Melt is to change from a solid to a liquid.

Start with Your Standards

Habits of Mind

S2CS3a. Use ordinary hand tools and instruments to construct, measure, and look at objects.

S2CS5b. Draw pictures (grade level appropriate) that correctly portray features of the thing being described.

Physical Science

S2P2a. Identify sources of light energy, heat energy, and energy of motion.

S2P2b. Describe how light, heat, and motion energy are used.

light
Light is a kind of energy you can see.

GEORGIA STANDARDS

S2CS3a. Use ordinary hand tools and instruments to construct, measure, and look at objects.
S2P2a. Identify sources of light energy, heat energy, and energy of motion.

? What Is Heat?

Science and You

Knowing about heat helps us control how hot things get.

Inquiry Skill

Measure You can use a thermometer to find out how warm or cold a place is.

What You Need

3 thermometers

Warm and Cool Places

Steps

STEP 1

Place	Warm or Cool?	Temperature

1. **Predict** Use a chart like the one shown. In the first column, list three places to measure temperature. In the second column, predict if each place will be warm or cool.

2. **Experiment** Place one thermometer in each place on your list.

STEP 2

3. **Measure** After five minutes, read each thermometer.

4. **Record Data** Write the temperature of each place in your chart.

STEP 3

Think and Share

1. **Compare** How did the temperatures you measured compare with your predictions?

2. **Infer** Why are some places warmer than others?

Guided Inquiry

Experiment Record the temperature of a thermometer. Then hold the bulb of the thermometer for one minute. Record the temperature and compare.

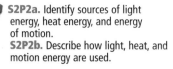
S2P2a. Identify sources of light energy, heat energy, and energy of motion.
S2P2b. Describe how light, heat, and motion energy are used.

Sources of Heat

Heat is a kind of energy that makes things warm. More heat makes things hot. Less heat makes things cool.

There are many sources of heat energy. The Sun is Earth's main source of heat energy. Most living things need energy from the Sun to survive.

▼ **Banks Lake National Wildlife Refuge, Georgia**

▲ Burning wood is a source of heat.

Other sources of heat energy are fuel such as wood and oil.

Heat energy also comes from objects such as lamps, heaters, stoves, and toasters.

🔘 **Main Idea and Details** What are three sources of heat?

▲ The toaster heats bread to make toast.

Express Lab

Activity Card 14
Make Heat

How Heat Is Used

People use heat energy in different ways. Heat is used to warm our homes and bodies. It is used to cook our food. We also use heat to dry our clothes and hair.

Heat from the hair dryer dries her hair.

Heat energy changes things. When you cook food, you end up with something different than what you started with. If something frozen is heated it melts. When things **melt** they change from a solid to a liquid.

▶ **Main Idea and Details** What are the uses of heat?

When heat is added to frozen soup it melts into a liquid.

Lesson Wrap-Up

❶ **Vocabulary** What happens when **heat** is added to something that is frozen?

❷ **Reading Skill** What are three ways people use heat?

❸ **Measure** When might you want to measure temperature?

🔦 **Technology** Visit **www.eduplace.com/gascp** to find out more about heat.

THE WARMING SUN

The Pueblo Indians used the Sun to heat their homes. The homes are built with adobe bricks. The bricks trap the Sun's heat during the day. At night the bricks give off stored heat. This heats the Pueblo Indian's homes all night.

Adobe bricks are made by mixing sand, soil, clay and water.

The Sun's heat dries the bricks.

STANDARDS S2P2b. Describe how light, heat, and motion energy are used.

SOCIAL STUDIES LINK

The floors of adobe homes were stacked so the Sun warms every level.

Sharing Ideas

1. **Write About It** How is the Sun used by the Pueblo Indians?

2. **Talk About It** How is the Sun different from other sources of heat?

Lesson 2

GEORGIA STANDARDS

S2CS5b. Draw pictures (grade level appropriate) that correctly portray features of the thing being described.
S2P2b. Describe how light, heat, and motion energy are used.

Essential Question: What Is Light?

Science and You

Light is needed to see the world around you.

Inquiry Skill

Experiment You can use items and plan steps to find out more about light energy.

What You Need

objects

index card

Seeing Things

Steps

1. Have a partner sit ten feet from a desk.

2. Write a secret word on an index card. Do not let anyone see your secret word.

3. As your partner looks away, place your card and objects in any order on the desk.

4. Turn out the lights. Have your partner draw the objects and your secret word.

5. Turn on the lights. Have your partner draw the objects and your secret word again.

STEP 3

STEP 4

Think and Share

1. **Compare** When was it easiest to read the secret word?

2. **Infer** How does the amount of light affect what you see?

Guided Inquiry

Experiment In a darkened room, shine a flashlight on the objects from ten feet, and twenty feet away. Compare how much detail you see.

Vocabulary

light

▶ **Reading Skill**

Cause and Effect

GPS **S2P2a.** Identify sources of light energy, heat energy, and energy of motion.
S2P2b. Describe how light, heat, and motion energy are used.

Sources of Light

There are many sources of light. **Light** is a kind of energy you can see. Earth gets light from the Sun. Think about the different light sources you use every day.

There is a lot of light on a sunny day.

Express Lab

Activity Card 15
Use Light to Communicate

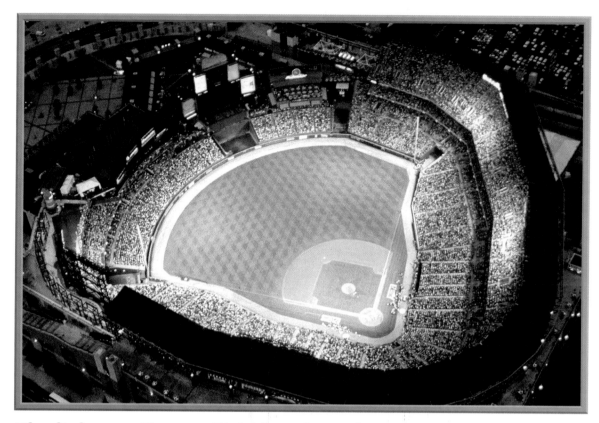

The lights at Turner Field let the Atlanta Braves play long after it is dark.

A burning candle gives off light. ▼

Fires, candles, and matches give off light when they burn. Light also comes from light bulbs inside flashlights, headlights, and lamps. You might even have some toys that make light.

▶ **Cause and Effect** **What are three sources of light?**

How Light Is Used

You need light for many things. Light from the Sun can change to heat. That is how the Sun heats Earth. Light also helps you see.

People use light to keep safe while driving or walking. Traffic lights let walkers and drivers know when to go and when to stop.

What lights up the city of Atlanta?

Saint Simons Island, Georgia

Lighthouses use light bulbs to send out powerful beams of light. Their light helps guide boats safely along rocky shores.

▶ **Cause and Effect** What would happen if a traffic light was broken?

Lesson Wrap-Up

❶ **Vocabulary** What is **light**?

❷ **Reading Skill** How do we use light?

❸ **Experiment** How could you find out which lamp would make the best reading light in a room?

Technology Visit **www.eduplace.com/gascp** to find out more about light energy.

EXTREME Science

LIGHT TRAP

STANDARDS S2P2a. Identify sources of light energy, heat energy, and energy of motion.

What is that tiny light dancing in the deep, dark ocean? Is it something to eat? If a fish gets too close, it will not find dinner. It will be dinner!

Meet the deep-sea anglerfish. This fish hunts with light. The female angler has a spine on her head that glows in the dark. The anglerfish wiggles the light to attract fish it catches.

Fireflies make light to find each other in the dark.

Wiggling Light on Spine

LIGHT EATER
The jaws and stomach of the anglerfish stretch so it can eat fish bigger than it is!

STANDARDS S2CS2a. Use whole numbers in ordering, counting, identifying, measuring and describing things and experiences.
M2D1a. Organize and display data using picture graphs, Venn diagrams, bar graphs, and simple charts/tables to record results.
ELA2W1a. Writes text of a length appropriate to address a topic and tell the story.

Math Compare and Order Numbers

Look at the list of light bulbs below. Compare the number of watts. Then record the numbers in a chart. List the bulbs in order from the greatest number of watts to the least.

Watts of Light Bulbs	
Light Bulb	Watts
Bulb A	90 Watts
Bulb B	150 Watts
Bulb C	60 Watts

 **Using Energy**

Every day, you use heat and light energy. Make a list of the heat and light sources you used today. Then write how each source is used.

 STANDARDS S2P2b. Describe how light, heat, and motion energy are used. **GeorgiaTask S2P2C.**

Energy Collage

Classify objects that give off heat, light, or both into three groups.

- Go on an energy walk. List objects that give off heat, light, or both.

- Find or draw pictures of objects on your list.

- Place each picture in the correct group.

- Share your collage with others.

Visual Summary

Heat and light are forms of energy that are used for many things.

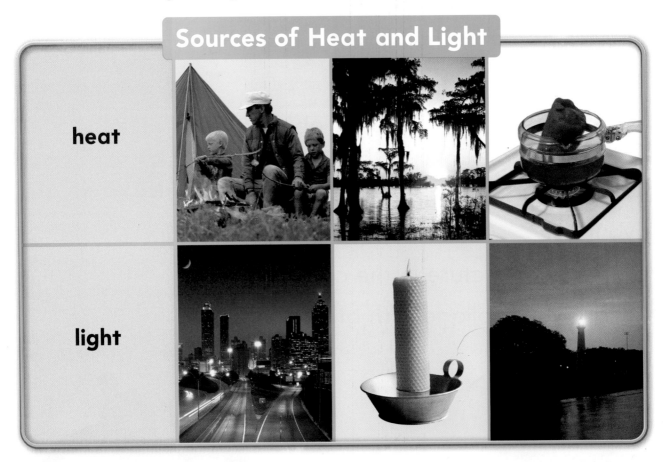

Sources of Heat and Light

heat

light

Main Ideas

1. What is Earth's main source of heat? **(p. 172)**   `S2P2a`

2. What are three sources of light in your home? **(p. 181)**   `S2P2a`

3. What are ways you use heat? **(p. 174–175)**   `S2P2b`

Vocabulary

Choose the correct word from the box.

4. A kind of energy that you can see

5. To change from a solid to a liquid

6. A kind of energy that makes things warm

S2CS7a

heat (p. 172)

melt (p. 175)

light (p. 180)

Using Science Skills

7. **Experiment** Plants need light to grow. How could you find the best place in your home for a plant? S2P2b

8. **Critical Thinking** Bread is baking in the oven. Why is the kitchen warmer than the other rooms? S2P2a

GPS CRCT Prep

9. Which object is NOT a source of heat and light?

the Sun   a lamp   a hair dryer

Ⓐ   Ⓑ   Ⓒ

S2P2a

GPS Test Practice

Choose the correct answer.

1. You can change the direction that a ball moves by giving it

a push.
Ⓐ

speed.
Ⓑ

mass.
Ⓒ

S2P3a

2. April broke her pencil. The pencil changed its

state.
Ⓐ

size.
Ⓑ

color.
Ⓒ

S2P1b

3. What is Earth's main source of light?

the Sun
Ⓐ

a lamp
Ⓑ

a candle
Ⓒ

S2P2a

4. Read the chart below to find the answer. The runners traveled at different

Runner	Time in Seconds	Distance in Meters
Kim	58	100
Max	63	100
Valentina	60	100

distances.
Ⓐ

speeds.
Ⓑ

paths.
Ⓒ

S2P3b

5. Motion is used to

see objects.   move objects.   change objects.

   Ⓐ   Ⓑ   Ⓒ

`S2P3a`

GPS Checking Main Ideas

Write the correct answer.

6. What is the difference between a solid and a liquid?   `S2P1a`

7. Which car is moving at a faster speed? How do you know?   `S2P3b`

FINISH

SPEEDY   RACER

STANDARDS S2CS4d. Compare very different sizes, weights, ages (baby/adult), and speeds (fast/slow) of both human made and natural made things.

You Can...

Discover More

What is the fastest speed that a human can run?

At the 1996 Olympics, a man ran 200 meters in 19.32 seconds. That's about 37 kilometers an hour. But compared with a cheetah, humans are slow. A cheetah can run three times as fast as a human, or almost 112 kilometers per hour!

 Go to **www.eduplace.com/gascp** to see animals and objects that move quickly and slowly.

GEORGIA SCIENCE

UNIT C

Life Science

Cricket Connection

Visit www.eduplace.com/gascp to check out *Click, Ask,* and *Odyssey* magazine articles and activities.

UNIT C

Life Science

Reading in Science 194

Science in Georgia:
Life Science Preview 196

Chapter 6
Plant Life Cycles 202

Chapter 7
Animal Life Cycles 242

Independent Reading

Marvelous
Mammals

Are They
Look-Alikes?

The Life
of a Bean

Georgia Fun Facts

BOING

Cougars have powerful hind legs. They can spring foward 30 feet in one leap.

Life Science

Plants and animals have life cycles that you can predict.

GPS STANDARDS ELA2R4a. Reads a variety of texts for information and pleasure.

Caterpillar

by Mary Dawson

Creepy crawly caterpillar
Looping up and down,
Furry tufts of hair along
Your back of golden brown.

You will soon be wrapped in silk,
Asleep for many a day;
And then, a handsome butterfly,
You'll stretch and fly away.

Science in Georgia

 STANDARDS S2L1b. Relate seasonal changes to observations of how a tree changes throughout a school year.

How Do Trees Change?

See how the silver maple tree changes each season in Clarke County, Georgia.

Golden Fall
This silver maple tree's colorful leaves drop to the ground.

Winter Buds
Look at the tiny
red buds start to grow.

Spring Fruits
The fruit is a winged
seed. It is carried by
the wind in late spring.

Summer Leaves
Green leaves grow on
the branches in summer.

Science in Georgia

GPS **STANDARDS S2L1b.** Relate seasonal changes to observations of how a tree changes throughout a school year.

The Longleaf Pine Tree

The longleaf pine tree changes in different ways from the silver maple tree. Compare how these two trees in the forest change.

This green cone will ripen, turn brown, and open.

After opening, this ripe cone drops its seeds in the fall.

Longleaf pine trees have needles. The needles stay green all year.

Choose the best answer.

1. How does a silver maple tree change in the winter?

   (A) It loses its fruit.

   (B) Its leaves turn green.

   (C) It grows red buds.

Performance Task

Compare Leaves

Collect leaves from different trees. Use paper and crayons to make leaf rubbings. Compare how the leaves are alike and different.

Hands-On Project

GPS **STANDARDS S2CS5b.** Draw pictures (grade level appropriate) that correctly portray features of the things being described. **GeorgiaTask S2L1A, S2L1E**

How Does a Tree Change?

How do trees change where you live? Choose a tree and observe it to see how it changes each season.

Step 1: Plan

- Choose a tree to observe.

Step 2: Do It

- Observe the tree once each month. Draw the tree. Then write the name of the month at the top of your paper.

- Write a sentence describing the tree.

- Do this every month.

- Put your pictures together to make a calendar.

December

The tree has no leaves.

Step 3: Communicate

- Share your calendar with a partner.

- Talk about how the tree changed throughout the year.

My Tree Calendar

Chapter 6

Plant Life Cycles

LESSON 1

Seeds form in fruits. How are seeds important to plants?

LESSON 2

Corn seeds come from a corn plant. What grows if you plant a corn seed?

LESSON 3

Not all daisies look alike. How might daisies in a field be different?

LESSON 4

This plant is growing toward the window. Why would this happen?

Vocabulary Preview

Vocabulary

flower p. 208

fruit p. 208

seed p. 208

life cycle p. 210

cone p. 212

inherit p. 218

environment p. 225

population p. 226

gravity p. 232

Picture Glossary p. H18

Vocabulary Skill

Use Syllables

environment

Break the word into syllables. Say each syllable aloud, clapping once for each syllable.

flower

A flower is a plant part where fruit and seeds form.

cone

A cone is the part where seeds form in a plant without flowers.

population

A population is a group of the same kind of living thing in one place.

environment

An environment is all the living and nonliving things around a living thing.

Georgia Performance Standards

Start with Your Standards

Habits of Mind

S2CS2a. Use whole numbers in ordering, counting, identifying, measuring, and describing things and experiences.

S2CS4c. Describe changes in the size, weight, color, or movement of things, and note which of their qualities remain the same during a specific change.

S2CS5c. Use simple pictographs and bar graphs to communicate data.

Life Science

S2L1c. Investigate the life cycle of a plant by growing a plant from a seed and by recording changes over a period of time.

S2L1d. Identify fungi (mushrooms) as living organisms.

GEORGIA STANDARDS

S2CS3a. Use ordinary hand tools and instruments to construct, measure, and look at objects.

S2L1c. Investigate the life cycle of a plant by growing a plant from a seed and by recording changes over a period of time.

? How Do Plants Change During Their Life Cycles?

Essential Question

Science and You

You know why seeds are important when you know about plant life cycles.

Inquiry Skill

Observe You can use a hand lens to see small objects or details.

What You Need

fruits

hand lens

crayons

Fruits and Seeds

Steps

STEP 1

① **Observe** Look at the outside of each fruit. Draw a picture of what you see. **Safety:** Do not eat the fruit!

② **Observe** Use a hand lens to look closely at the inside of each fruit. Draw a picture of what you see. **Safety:** Wash your hands!

STEP 2

③ **Communicate** Share your drawings with others. Talk about what you saw.

Think and Share

1. **Compare** How were all the fruits alike?

STEP 3

2. **Infer** What would you find if you cut open a different fruit?

Guided Inquiry

Experiment Think of some seeds that you can open with your fingers. Open them. Observe and record what is inside. Compare what is inside different seeds.

Vocabulary

flower

fruit

seed

life cycle

cone

Reading Skill

Sequence

```
┌─────────────────┐
│                 │
└─────────────────┘
        ↓
┌─────────────────┐
│                 │
└─────────────────┘
        ↓
┌─────────────────┐
│                 │
└─────────────────┘
```

S2L1c. Investigate the life cycle of a plant by growing a plant from a seed and by recording changes over a period of time.

Plant Parts

A plant has many parts. Some parts help a plant make new plants. A **flower** is the plant part where fruit and seeds form. A **fruit** is the part of a flower that is around a seed. A **seed** is the part from which a new plant grows.

Pea Plant

Inside a seed is a new plant and the food it needs to grow.

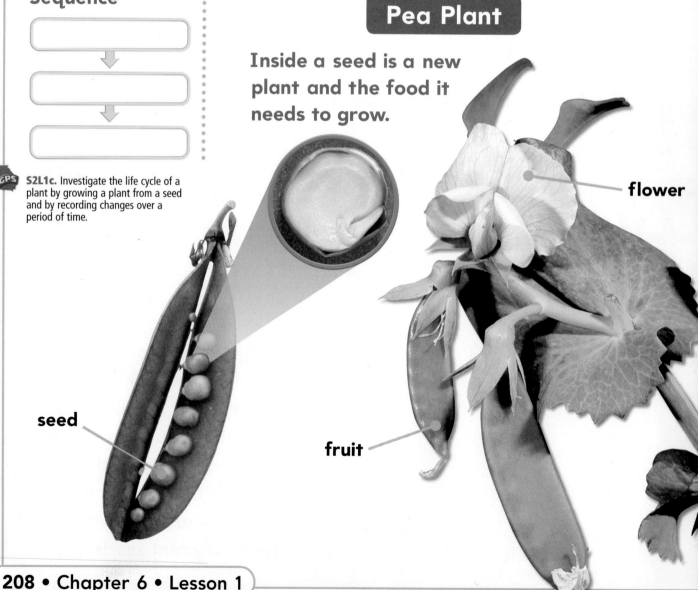

flower

seed

fruit

Pea plants and almond trees have flowers. Both kinds of flowers have seeds inside. The flowers dry up after the fruit and seeds form. The fruits grow bigger. If the seeds are planted in soil, they can grow into new plants.

▶ **Sequence** What happens after the fruit and seeds form?

flower

Sweet Almond Tree

fruit

seed

Express Lab

Activity Card 16
Order a Plant Life Cycle

Plant Life Cycles

All living things grow, change, and finally die. The series of changes that a living thing goes though as it grows is its **life cycle**.

Different kinds of plants have different life cycles. Most plants start from a seed. When the seed gets what it needs, it starts to grow.

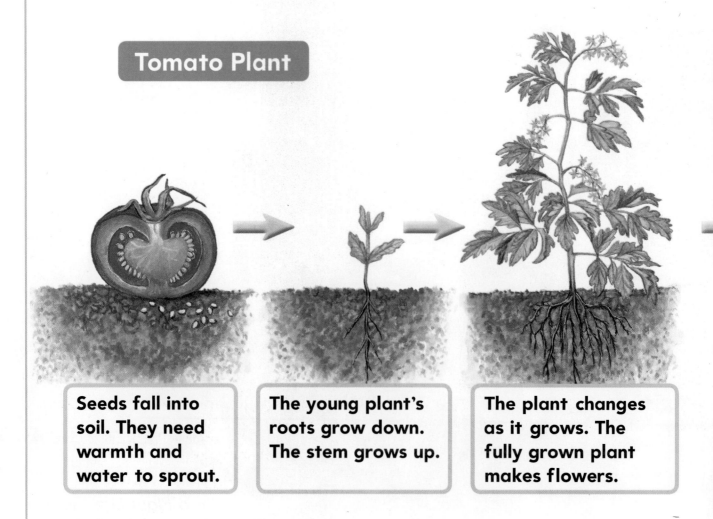

Tomato Plant

Seeds fall into soil. They need warmth and water to sprout.

The young plant's roots grow down. The stem grows up.

The plant changes as it grows. The fully grown plant makes flowers.

The plant grows and changes. It grows more stems and leaves. It grows flowers that make new seeds and fruit. New plants can grow from the seeds. These plants will look like the parent plant from which they came. The cycle of growing and changing starts again.

▶ **Sequence** When does a seed start to grow?

Flowers make fruit. Seeds grow inside the fruit.

The parent plant dies. The seeds may scatter. They may grow into new plants.

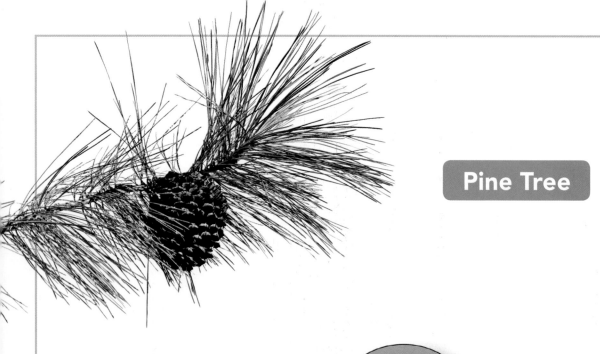

Pine Tree

| Pine seeds grow in a cone. | A seed grows into a young plant called a seedling. |

Life Cycle of a Pine Tree

Not all plants have flowers and fruits. Some plants have cones. A **cone** is the part where seeds form in plants without flowers. The cone protects the seeds while they grow.

▶ **Sequence** How does a pine tree change as it grows?

| The seedling grows into a tree. | The tree grows and cones form. | The life cycle begins again with new seeds. |

Lesson Wrap-Up

❶ Vocabulary What is a **seed**?

❷ Reading Skill What stage comes after the seed in a plant's life cycle?

❸ Observe How does a hand lens help you observe seeds?

Technology Visit **www.eduplace.com/gascp** to find out more about plant life cycles.

Marvelous Mushrooms

Is that *smoke*? No, these funny looking bulbs are mushrooms called puffballs. They puff out clouds of dust-like spores that grow new mushrooms. Mushrooms may look like plants, but they are not. Mushrooms do not need sunlight to grow. They do not make their own food, like plants do. Mushrooms are part of a group of living things called fungi.

Danger!
Some mushrooms are safe to eat. These galerina mushrooms are not! They are very poisonous. Never eat or touch any wild mushroom you find.

spores

Lesson 2

GPS GEORGIA STANDARDS

S2CS4c. Describe changes in the size, weight, color, or movement of things, and note which of their other qualities remain the same during a specific change.
S2L1c. Investigate the life cycle of a plant by growing a plant from a seed and by recording changes over a period of time.

What Kind of a Plant Grows from a Seed?

Science and You

You know different types of seeds grow into different types of plants.

Inquiry Skill

Compare Tell how objects or events are alike and different.

What You Need

goggles

seeds

cup and soil

water and ruler

Plant Seeds

Steps

1. Choose one kind of seed. Look at the picture on the packet. Plant several seeds in soil. Water as needed. **Safety:** Wear goggles!

STEP 1

2. **Observe** Watch for a plant to start to grow. Draw that plant every day. Use a chart like the one shown.

STEP 2

Plant Growth

Date	Date	Date	Date	Date
Height	Height	Height	Height	Height
Date	Date	Date	Date	Date
Height	Height	Height	Height	Height

3. **Measure** Measure your plant every day. Record its height below each drawing. **Safety:** Wash your hands!

STEP 3

Think and Share

1. **Compare** How is your plant like the plant pictured on the seed packet? How is it different?

2. **Infer** Why does your plant look like the one on the seed packet?

Guided Inquiry

Ask Questions Think about how plants are alike and different. Ask: What if I planted a _____ seed? Predict what would happen.

▶ **Vocabulary**

inherit

▶ **Reading Skill**

Draw Conclusions

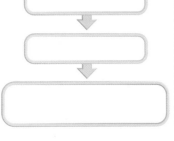

GPS **S2L1c.** Investigate the life cycle of a plant by growing a plant from a seed and by recording changes over a period of time.

Plants and Their Parents

New plants grow from the seeds of the parent plant. The new plant inherits traits from the parent plant. All living things **inherit**, or have passed on to them, traits from their parents.

Some traits that a plant may inherit are color, shape, or size. The new plant will have the same leaf shape as the parent plant. It will grow the same kind of fruit. The new plant may be the same color as the parent plant. It may grow to be the same size.

When new poppies grow, they look like the parent plants.

How Plants Compare

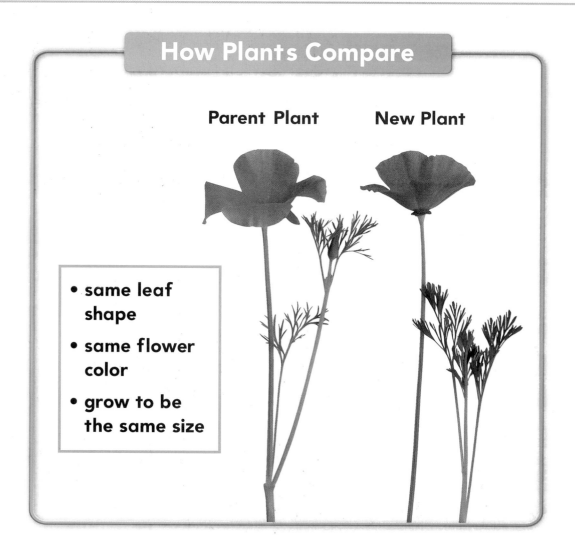

Parent Plant New Plant

- same leaf shape
- same flower color
- grow to be the same size

▶ **Draw Conclusions** In what ways might a new tulip plant be like its parent plant?

Express Lab

Activity Card 17
*Compare Young Plants
to Their Parents*

Oak Trees and Acorns

Acorns are the fruit of an oak tree. When acorns fall to the ground, the seeds inside may grow into new plants.

acorns

Blue Oak Tree

The new plants look like one another and like the parent plant. They are all oak trees. They all inherit the same flat leaves. Like their parent, the new oak plants may someday form acorns. The seeds inside the acorns may grow into new oak trees.

new oak trees

▶ **Draw Conclusions** What kinds of plants always grow from acorns?

Lesson Wrap-Up

❶ **Vocabulary** What do new plants **inherit**?

❷ **Reading Skill** What would the seeds of a maple tree grow into?

❸ **Compare** How is a new plant like its parent plant?

Technology Visit **www.eduplace.com/gascp** to find out more about plants.

Lesson 3

GPS GEORGIA STANDARDS

S2CS5c. Use simple pictographs and bar graphs to communicate data.
S2L1c. Investigate the life cycle of a plant by growing a plant from a seed and by recording changes over a period of time.

Essential Question

How Do Plants of the Same Kind Differ?

Science and You

Plants of the same kind are not exactly alike. They are different enough you can tell them apart.

Inquiry Skill

Use Numbers Use numbers to describe and compare objects.

What You Need

4 pea pods

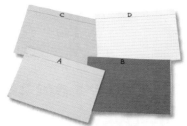

4 index cards

crayons and ruler

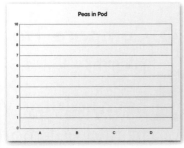

bar graph

Compare Pea Pods

Steps

1 **Measure** Put a pea pod on each index card. Measure the length of each pod in centimeters. Record your data on the cards.

2 **Record Data** Open pod **A**. Count the number of peas. Record the number on the card. Repeat for each pod.

3 **Use Numbers** Complete the bar graph. Add labels. Use the data on the cards to graph the number of peas in each pod.

Think and Share

1. **Use Numbers** How do the lengths of the pods compare? How do the number of peas compare?

2. **Predict** What do you think you would find if you looked at four more pea pods? Tell why.

STEP 1

STEP 2

STEP 3

Peas in Pod

Habits of Mind

Guided Inquiry

Experiment Measure the length of three bananas or apples. Use a balance to measure the mass of each fruit. How are fruits of the same kind different?

Vocabulary

environment

population

▶ **Reading Skill**
Compare and Contrast

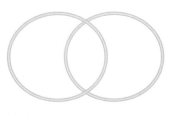

S2L1c. Investigate the life cycle of a plant by growing a plant from a seed and by recording changes over a period of time.

The Same but Different

You learned that new plants inherit traits from the parent plant. The new plants often look like the parents and one another.

But new plants that grow from seeds from the same parent are not exactly alike. The new plants may be different because they may inherit different traits. Their size may be different. They may even be a different color.

Seeds from a red raspberry plant may produce new plants that make red or gold raspberries.

What might cause these two new plants to look different?

There are other reasons that new plants from the same parents may look different. The plants may be affected by their environment.

An **environment** is all the living and nonliving things around a living thing. A new plant that does not get the right amount of sunlight may not grow as well as others.

▶ **Compare and Contrast** In what ways can new plants from the same parents differ?

Express Lab

Activity Card 18
Compare Leaf Size

Differences in a Bigger Group

You can see differences among plants from the same parents. <u>You can see even more differences among plants of a population.</u> A **population** is a group of the same kind of living thing in one place.

All the petunia plants in a garden make up a population. The plants may inherit different traits. They may have flowers of different shapes and colors, but they are all part of the same population. They are all petunias.

a population of petunias

Each daffodil inherited different traits from its parent plants.

Plants in a population can also look different because they are affected by their environment. A plant that has more space will grow better than one that is crowded. Plants that get too much water will not grow well.

How are these plants affected by their environment?

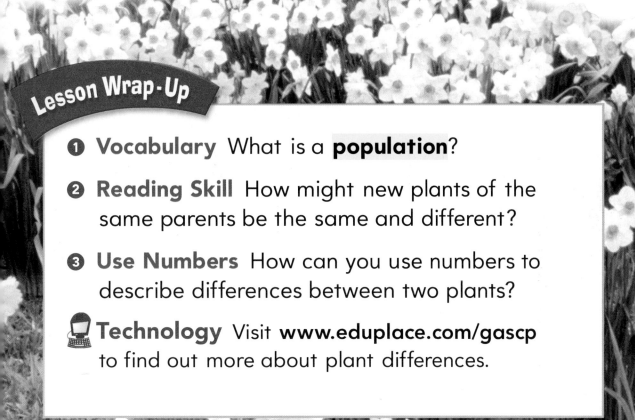

▶ **Compare and Contrast** How might plants of a population be the same and different?

Lesson Wrap-Up

❶ **Vocabulary** What is a **population**?

❷ **Reading Skill** How might new plants of the same parents be the same and different?

❸ **Use Numbers** How can you use numbers to describe differences between two plants?

🖥 **Technology** Visit **www.eduplace.com/gascp** to find out more about plant differences.

Great Grapes

In the 1870s, William Thompson and his son, George, grew the first seedless grapes in Yuba County, California. People liked the seedless grapes. Since then, grape growers have created many kinds of seedless grapes.

Grape growers choose plants with the traits that people like. Growers use seeds or stem cuttings from those plants to grow new plants. The new plants inherit traits from the parent plants.

Most California raisins are made from Thompson seedless grapes.

GPS STANDARDS S2L1c. Investigate the life cycle of a plant by growing a plant from a seed and by recording changes over a period of time.

READING **LINK**

All of the seedless grapes in California are offspring of the grapes that Thompson grew in the 1870s. Red Flame seedless grapes were created by combining Thompson seedless grapes with some other kinds of grapes.

Sharing Ideas

1. **Write About It** How do grape growers create new kinds of grapes?

2. **Talk About It** Describe a new kind of fruit that you would like to grow. What traits would it have?

229

Lesson 4

 GEORGIA STANDARDS

S2CS2a. Use whole numbers in ordering, counting, identifying, measuring, and describing things and experiences.
S2L1c. Investigate the life cycle of a plant by growing a plant from a seed and by recording changes over a period of time.

How Do Plants React to Their Environment?

Essential Question

Science and You

A plant's environment can affect the way it grows. This helps you know where to place plants so they will grow better.

Inquiry Skill

Record Data You can write or draw what happens first, next, and last.

What You Need

seeds

2 plastic bags and paper towels

thermometer and water

Seed Growth			
Day	Temperature in Refrigerator	Temperature in Closet	Observations

chart

Sprouting Seeds

Steps

1. Put a wet paper towel and four seeds in each bag. Put one bag in a refrigerator. Put the other bag in a dark closet.

2. **Measure** Measure the temperature of the air next to each bag. Record the data in a chart.

3. **Record Data** Observe the seeds. Record in the chart what you see.

4. Repeat steps 2 and 3 every day for one week.

STEP 1

STEP 2

STEP 3

Seed Growth			
Day	Temperature in Refrigerator	Temperature in Closet	Observations
Monday	5°C	20°C	

Think and Share

1. **Compare** Which seeds sprouted and grew faster?

2. **Predict** What might happen if you moved the seeds that were in the refrigerator to the closet?

Guided Inquiry

Experiment Think of a plan to compare how plants grow in different amounts of light. Tell your plan to a classmate. Have the classmate follow your plan.

GPS **S2L1c.** Investigate the life cycle of a plant by growing a plant from a seed and by recording changes over a period of time.

S2E3a. Recognize effects that occur in a specific area caused by weather, plants, animals, and/or people.

Gravity, Light, and Touch

Plants are affected by gravity, light, and touch. **Gravity** is a force that pulls all objects toward each other.

The roots of a plant grow down toward the pull of gravity. As the roots grow down into the soil, the plant gets the water it needs. The stems of a plant grow up, away from the pull of gravity.

How is this tree affected by gravity?

A mimosa plant reacts to the touch of a pencil.

Some plants are affected by touch. A mimosa plant closes its leaves when it is touched. It protects itself from danger. When insects crawl on the leaves, the leaves close. The insects cannot eat the leaves and go away.

A plant needs sunlight to make food. So the stem of a plant grows toward the light. People sometimes turn their houseplants a little each day. This helps the stems grow straight.

How is this plant affected by light?

▶ **Cause and Effect** How does gravity affect plants?

Express Lab

Activity Card 19
Compare Temperature

233

Weather Affects Plants

Weather can affect how plants grow. Air temperature, wind, and rainfall all affect plant growth.

Strong, sudden wind can cause trees and crops to fall over. Wind might also pull some plants out of the soil. Steady winds can change the shape of a growing tree over time.

This pine tree in the Sierra Nevada mountains was affected by the wind.

If the temperature gets too hot or too cold, plants can be injured or die. Very hot weather can cause plants to stop growing.

The wrong amount of water can affect how plants grow. If there is too little rain, seeds will not start to grow. If there is too much rain, a plant's roots might rot.

A quick drop in temperature injured this plant.

▶ **Cause and Effect** How can **weather** affect how plants grow?

Lesson Wrap-Up

① **Vocabulary** What is **gravity**?

② **Reading Skill** How does light affect how plants grow?

③ **Record Data** How can you record data about how light affects plants?

Technology Visit **www.eduplace.com/gascp** to find out more about plant growth.

GPS **STANDARDS S2CS2a.** Use whole numbers in ordering, counting, identifying, measuring, and describing things and experiences. **M2N5** Students will represent and interpret quantities and relationships using mathematical expressions including equality and inequality signs (=, <, >). **ELA2W1b.** Use traditional organizational patterns for conveying information (e.g., chronological order, similarity and difference, answering questions).

Math Compare Seeds

Keesha and Mark each have a pumpkin. They open the pumpkins and count the seeds inside. The chart shows their results.

Pumpkin Seeds	
Child	Number of Seeds
Keesha	85
Mark	62

1. Compare the number of seeds. Use < or > to write a number sentence.

2. Whose pumpkin has more seeds? How many more seeds does it have?

 **Describe a Plant**

Write about a plant. Tell how the plant changes as it grows. Start with a seed. Draw pictures to go with your story. Share your story with the class.

How My Seed Grows

Georgia

 STANDARDS S2L1c. Investigate the life cycle of a plant by growing a plant from a seed and by recording changes over a period of time.

How do growing plants change?

- Draw each stage of the life cycle of a plant on a card.

- On the back, describe each stage.

- Mix up your cards. Trade cards with a partner and place them in order.

STANDARDS S2CS6d. All different kinds of people can be and are scientists.

Botanist

A botanist is a scientist who studies plants. Some botanists try to grow new kinds of plants. Some look for new plants in the wild.

Some botanists work with farmers. They look for ways to keep harmful insects away from plants. They also find ways for farmers to grow more crops.

What It Takes!

- At least four years of college
- An interest in science and plants

Georgia

 STANDARDS S2CS6d. All different kinds of people can be and are scientists.

Tracey Troutman

Agriculture is the science of raising plants and animals for food and other uses. Tracey Troutman studies agriculture at the University of Georgia. For her career, she wants to use science to help farmers.

Tracey worked one summer in Europe. Her job was to tell people in other countries about foods that grow on Georgia farms.

Tracey has studied new ways to raise chickens. Tracey grew up in Rochelle, Georgia where there are many farms.

239

Visual Summary

The way plants grow and change depends on the parent plants and the environment.

Seeds form in fruits.

Plants inherit many traits from the parents.

Plants Grow and Change

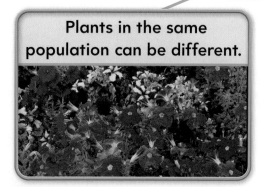

Plants in the same population can be different.

Plants are affected by their environment.

Main Ideas

1. What are three parts of a plant that help make new plants? (p. 208)   S2L1c

2. List two reasons why new plants with the same parents might be different. (pp. 224–225)   S2L1c

3. Explain why the roots of a bush grow down and its stem grows up. (pp. 232–233)   S2L1c

Vocabulary

Choose the correct word from the box.

4. A plant part where fruit and seeds form

5. All the living and nonliving things around a living thing

6. The part of a flower that is around a seed

flower (p. 208)

fruit (p. 208)

environment (p. 225)

Using Science Skills

7. Describe the stages of a plant's life cycle. `S2L1c`

8. **Critical Thinking** A new tree and its parent plant have the same color bark. Tell why. `S2L1c`

 ## CRCT Prep

Choose the letter that best answers the question.

9. Two weeks of heavy rains flooded a tomato field. The tomato plants

died.	did not change.	grew.
Ⓐ	Ⓑ	Ⓒ

`S2L1c`

Chapter 7

Animal Life Cycles

LESSON 1

These chicks look alike. How are they like their parents?

LESSON 2

A caterpillar changes as it grows. How does it change?

LESSON 3

This dog can fetch. Why can some dogs do tricks?

LESSON 4

These hamsters are alike in many ways. How are they different?

Vocabulary Preview

Vocabulary

reproduce p. 248

offspring p. 248

adult p. 249

larva p. 256

pupa p. 256

learned p. 264

individual p. 271

Picture Glossary p. H18

Vocabulary Skill
Use What's Before

reproduce

The prefix **re-** means again. **Produce** means to make. So reproduce means to make again.

larva

A larva is the worm-like stage in an insect's life cycle.

pupa

A pupa is the stage when an insect changes form.

learned

Traits that are learned are not passed on from parents to their offspring.

reproduce

When living things reproduce, they make more living things of the same kind.

Georgia
Performance Standards

Start with Your Standards

Habits of Mind

S2CS4d. Compare very different sizes, weights, ages (baby/adult), and speeds (fast/slow) of both human made and natural things.

S2CS5a. Describe and compare things in terms of number, shape, texture, size, weight, color, and motion.

The Nature of Science

S2CS6a. When science investigation is done the way it was done before, we expect to get a similar result.

Life Science

S2L1a. Determine the sequence of the life cycle of common animals in your area: a mammal such as a cat or dog or classroom pet, a bird such as a chicken, an amphibian such as a frog, and an insect such as a butterfly.

Lesson 1

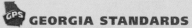

GEORGIA STANDARDS

S2CS4d. Compare very different sizes, weights, ages (baby/adult), and speeds (fast/slow) of both human made and natural things.

S2L1a. Determine the sequence of the life cycle of common animals in your area: a mammal such as a cat or dog or classroom pet, a bird such as a chicken, an amphibian such as a frog, and an insect such as a butterfly.

? Essential Question: Which Baby Animals Look Like Their Parents?

Science and You

Knowing which animals look like their parents helps you know what some baby animals will look like when they get older.

Inquiry Skill

Classify Sort living things into groups to show how they are alike.

What You Need

animal cards

Compare Life Cycles

Steps

① **Observe** Look at the animal pictures. Name the animals.

② **Classify** Think about how the animal pictures are alike and different. Sort the pictures. Make a group for each kind of animal.

③ **Order** each group. Put the baby first and the adult animal last.

④ **Record Data** Choose one group. Use the pictures to write about or draw the life cycle of that animal.

STEP 1

STEP 2

STEP 3

Think and Share

1. **Compare** How are the baby and adult in each group alike?

2. How do some animals change from babies to adults?

Guided Inquiry

Ask Questions Write three questions about how animals grow and change. Work together with classmates to find the answers.

▶ **Vocabulary**

reproduce
offspring
adult

▶ **Reading Skill**
Compare and
Contrast

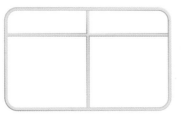

GPS **S2L1a.** Determine the sequence of
the life cycle of common animals in
your area: a mammal such as a cat or
dog or classroom pet, a bird such as a
chicken, an amphibian such as a frog,
and an insect such as a butterfly.

Adults and Offspring

All living things grow, change, and reproduce. When living things **reproduce**, they make more living things of the same kind.

Offspring are the living things that come from a living thing. Mammals, birds, fish, and reptiles have offspring that look very much like their parents. Offspring of other animals will look more like their parents as they grow.

Baby rabbits look very much like their parents.

adult and baby
tortoises

Offspring grow and change during their lives. A baby penguin will become a full grown penguin. An animal that is full grown is an **adult**. Then it will be about the same size and color as its parent. The series of changes that an animal goes through as it grows is its life cycle.

adult and baby penguins

▶ **Compare and Contrast** How are parents and offspring alike and different?

How do this adult and baby orca whale look alike?

Express Lab

Activity Card 20
Match Animals

249

Life Cycle of a Bird

A mother bird lays eggs. A chick grows inside each one.

A chick hatches from an egg. A parent feeds it.

Life Cycle of a Mouse

A mother mouse gives birth to baby mice.

The mother's body makes milk. The babies drink the milk.

Familiar Life Cycles

The stages in a life cycle are different for different animals. A mouse is a mammal. A mammal is born alive. A bird hatches from an egg. Baby birds and baby mice are much like their parents.

▶ **Compare and Contrast** How are the life cycles of a bird and a mouse the same?

The chick gets new feathers as it grows.

The young bird grows to be an adult. It can reproduce.

The mice grow more fur. They get bigger.

This mouse is fully grown. As an adult, it can reproduce.

Lesson Wrap-Up

❶ **Vocabulary** What is an **offspring**?

❷ **Reading Skill** How is the life cycle of a bird different from that of a mouse?

❸ **Classify** How could you sort animals by their life cycles?

Technology Visit **www.eduplace.com/gascp** to find out more about animal life cycles.

GEORGIA STANDARDS

S2CS4d. Compare very different sizes, weights, ages (baby/adult), and speeds (fast/slow) of both human made and natural things.

S2L1a. Determine the sequence of the life cycle of common animals in your area: a mammal such as a cat or dog or classroom pet, a bird such as a chicken, an amphibian such as a frog, and an insect such as a butterfly.

Essential Question

Which Baby Animals Look Unlike Their Parents?

Science and You

Knowing how some animals change will help you understand that a caterpillar and a moth are the same animal.

Inquiry Skill

Use Data You can use what you observe and record to learn more about something.

What You Need

Triops tank

Triops eggs

hand lens

ruler

Triops Stages

Steps

1. Gently pour the Triops eggs into a tank of water.
   Safety: Wash your hands!

STEP 1

2. **Observe** Use a hand lens to observe the Triops each day. Draw what they look like.

STEP 2

3. **Measure** When a Triops is three days old, measure its length. Repeat each day for five days. Record each day's data in a table.

STEP 3

Length of Triops	
Day 1	about _____ cm
Day 2	about _____ cm
Day 3	about _____ cm
Day 4	about _____ cm
Day 5	about _____ cm

Think and Share

1. **Use Data** How did the Triops change over time?

2. **Infer** How is a baby Triops different from its parents?

Guided Inquiry

Ask Questions Look at a partner's chart. Compare your data. If your data is different, ask questions about why your data is different.

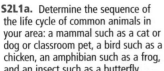

S2L1a. Determine the sequence of the life cycle of common animals in your area: a mammal such as a cat or dog or classroom pet, a bird such as a chicken, an amphibian such as a frog, and an insect such as a butterfly.

Vocabulary

larva

pupa

Reading Skill

Sequence

[ ]
↓
[ ]
↓
[ ]

Frog Life Cycle

Some young animals look very different from their parents. These animals change form as they grow to be adults.

Most amphibians change form as they grow. When they become adults, they will look like their parents.

Life Cycle of a Frog

A frog lays its eggs in water.

A tadpole hatches from an egg. It has gills, a tail, and no legs.

Over many weeks, a tadpole's back legs grow. Its skin gets thicker.

A frog is an amphibian. When frogs hatch from eggs, they have body parts that help them live in water.

Later, frogs grow parts that will help them live on land. Parts that they needed to live in water disappear. When frogs become adults, they look like their parents.

▶ **Sequence** What happens after parts for living on land form?

Lungs grow and gills disappear. The tail will soon disappear.

The tadpole grows to be an adult frog. An adult frog can reproduce.

Express Lab

Activity Card 21
Measure How a Frog Changes

A butterfly lays eggs on a plant.

A larva hatches from an egg. It eats the plant it is on.

A pupa does not eat. Wings and legs are forming.

Butterfly Life Cycle

Butterflies are insects. Most insects change form as they grow. The first stage in the life cycle of most insects is the egg. A larva hatches from the egg. A **larva** is the worm-like stage in an insect's life cycle. It looks very different from its parents.

A larva grows and sheds its skin many times. Then it turns into a pupa. A **pupa** is the stage when an insect changes form.

The change is finished. The pupa has become a butterfly.

A butterfly lives for several weeks. It lays eggs, and a new life cycle begins.

▶ **Sequence** What stage follows the larva stage?

Lesson Wrap-Up

❶ **Vocabulary** What is a **larva**?

❷ **Reading Skill** What happens before a tadpole's back legs grow?

❸ **Use Data** How is the data that you collect about life cycles useful?

🖳 **Technology** Visit **www.eduplace.com/gascp** to find out more about animals that change form.

EXTREME Science

STANDARDS S2CS5a. Describe and compare things in terms of number, shape, texture, size, weight, color, and motion.

Check Out These Chickens

Have you ever seen chickens like these? These chickens aren't wearing funny hats! They are bred to have certain traits, such as fluffy, curly feathers.

Breeders choose adult chickens with unusual colors or feathers to reproduce. Offspring that have those traits are chosen to reproduce again. Over time, the traits become common in that group.

This breed of Polish hen has been raised for the last 500 years.

This hen has head feathers like her father and body feathers like her mother.

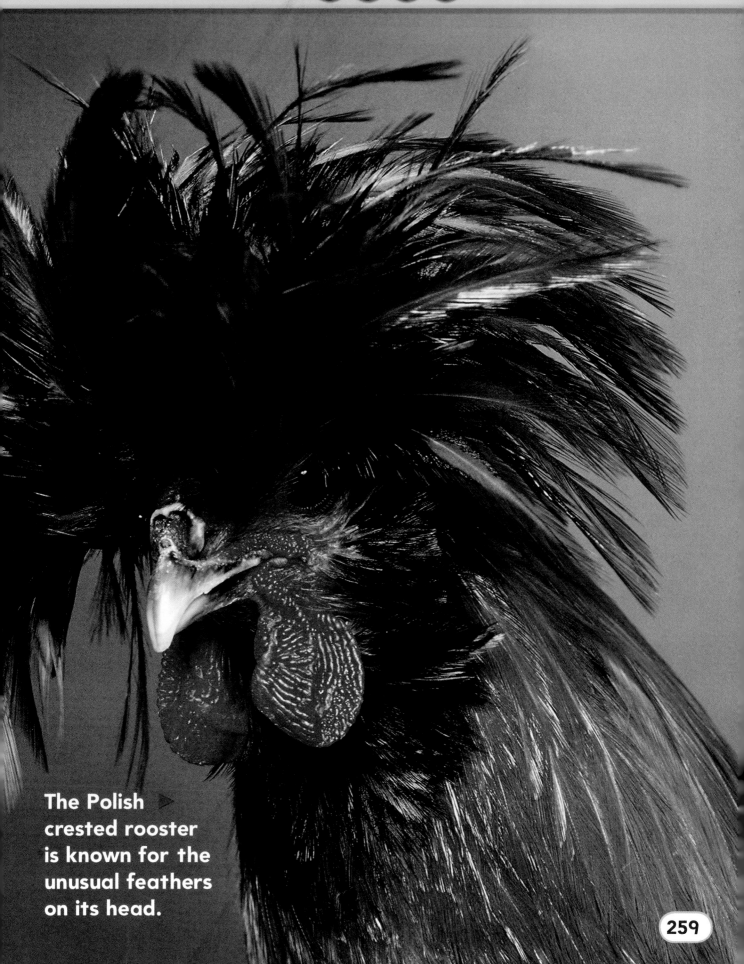

The Polish ▶ crested rooster is known for the unusual feathers on its head.

259

GPS GEORGIA STANDARDS

S2CS6a. When a science investigation is done the way it was done before, we expect to get a similar result.

S2L1a. Determine the sequence of the life cycle of common animals in your area: a mammal such as a cat or dog or classroom pet, a bird such as a chicken, an amphibian such as a frog, and an insect such as a butterfly.

Where Do Animals Get Their Traits?

Science and You

Animals inherit many traits from their parents. Some traits are learned or caused by the environment.

Inquiry Skill

Predict Instead of guessing, use patterns you observe to tell what you think will happen.

What You Need

goldfish

pencil

fish food

Train Goldfish

Steps

1. **Experiment** Use a pencil to gently tap a signal at one end of a fish tank. Watch and record what the fish do. Feed the fish at the other end of the tank.

STEP 1

2. **Record Data** Repeat Step 1 for the next three days. Watch and record what the fish do.

STEP 2

3. **Predict** On the fifth day, predict what the fish will do when you tap on the tank. Test your prediction, but do not feed the fish. Watch and record the actions of the fish.

STEP 3

Think and Share

1. **Infer** How did using the signal when you fed the fish help train them?

2. **Predict** What might happen if you tried this with different fish?

Guided Inquiry

Experiment Think about ways to train other animals. Make a plan. Communicate your plan with classmates.

261

Vocabulary

learned

▶ **Reading Skill**
Draw Conclusions

S2L1a. Determine the sequence of the life cycle of common animals in your area: a mammal such as a cat or dog or classroom pet, a bird such as a chicken, an amphibian such as a frog, and an insect such as a butterfly.

Inherited Traits

Just as new plants inherit traits from their parent plants, young animals inherit traits from their parents. When living things reproduce, they make more living things of the same kind.

When dogs reproduce, they always give birth to puppies. Cats always give birth to kittens, not puppies.

These kittens inherited their body shape from their parents.

How are these children like their parents?

People always give birth to children. Children of the same parents often look alike. They are all children in the same family, but they are all different from one another. They may have different eye or hair color. The shape of their noses may not be the same.

▶ **Draw Conclusions** Why might a brother and sister have the same ear shape?

Activity Card 22
Observe a Learned Behavior

Learned Traits

Some traits are learned. Traits that are **learned** are not passed on from parents to their offspring. You were not born knowing how to read. Reading is something that is learned.

Like you, animals also learn things as they live. These learned traits will not be passed on to their offspring.

This skunk learned where to find food.

Border collie herding sheep

Some animals are trained to help people. Different animals are trained to do different things.

This monkey has learned to use a CD player.

▶ **Draw Conclusions** Where might a dog get its traits?

Lesson Wrap-Up

❶ **Vocabulary** Name a trait that is **learned**.

❷ **Reading Skill** Why might kittens be the same color as their mother?

❸ **Predict** What kind of animal will a dog give birth to?

📱 **Technology** Visit **www.eduplace.com/gascp** to find out more about learned and inherited traits.

Spin a Yarn

How could you make a sweater that will last for 100 years? You would use yarn made from the hair, or fibers, of an alpaca.

Alpaca fibers are shiny, soft, and fine. This makes the fibers easy to spin into yarn. Alpaca yarn is lighter and stronger than yarn made from sheep's wool.

Most alpacas live in South America. Some live in the United States.

STANDARDS S2CS5a. Describe and compare things in terms of number, shape, texture, size, weight, color, and motion.

READING L I N K

Alpaca yarn is made from alpaca fibers of different colors.

Alpaca fibers come in more colors than any other animal fibers. There are more than 22 colors, even dark red! Breeders choose alpacas for their colors. So when these alpacas reproduce, the offspring may be the colors the breeders like. Some offspring may be different colors. Then there can be more colors of yarn.

Sharing Ideas

1. **Write About It** Make a list of traits that breeders might want in alpaca fibers.

2. **Talk About It** How is knowing about inherited traits helpful to alpaca breeders?

GPS GEORGIA STANDARDS

S2CS5c. Use simple pictographs and bar graphs to communicate data.
S2L1a. Determine the sequence of the life cycle of common animals in your area: a mammal such as a cat or dog or classroom pet, a bird such as a chicken, an amphibian such as a frog, and an insect such as a butterfly.

Essential Question ? How Do Animals of the Same Kind Differ?

Science and You

Living things of the same kind look very much alike. They are different enough you can tell them apart.

Inquiry Skill

Measure Use tools and metric units to find length.

What You Need

ruler

paper and pencil

graph

Measure Handspans

Steps

1 **Measure** Spread your fingers and place your hand on a sheet of paper. Draw lines at the end of your little finger and at the end of your thumb. Measure the distance between the two marks. Record your handspan measurement.

2 **Use Numbers** Survey your classmates. Find out each child's handspan. Record data on a tally chart like the one shown.

3 **Record Data** Use data from the tally chart to complete the bar graph. Add labels.

STEP 1

STEP 2

Handspans

Measurement	Number of Children
13 Centimeters	
14 Centimeters	
15 Centimeters	
16 Centimeters	
17 Centimeters	
18 Centimeters	
19 Centimeters	

STEP 3

Handspans of Classmates

Think and Share

1. **Use Numbers** What were the smallest and largest measurements?

2. **Compare** How are hands alike and different?

Guided Inquiry

Experiment Make a plan to compare foot lengths. Use numbers to compare foot measurements to handspan measurements.

▶ **Vocabulary**

individual

▶ **Reading Skill**
Main Idea and
Details

S2L1a. Determine the sequence of
the life cycle of common animals in
your area: a mammal such as a cat or
dog or classroom pet, a bird such as a
chicken, an amphibian such as a frog,
and an insect such as a butterfly.

Families Differ

Young animals in a family often look like their parents and one another. But the animals in a family are not exactly alike. Each animal inherits slightly different traits from its parents. The color or size of each animal may be different. They may even act in different ways.

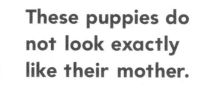

These puppies do not look exactly like their mother.

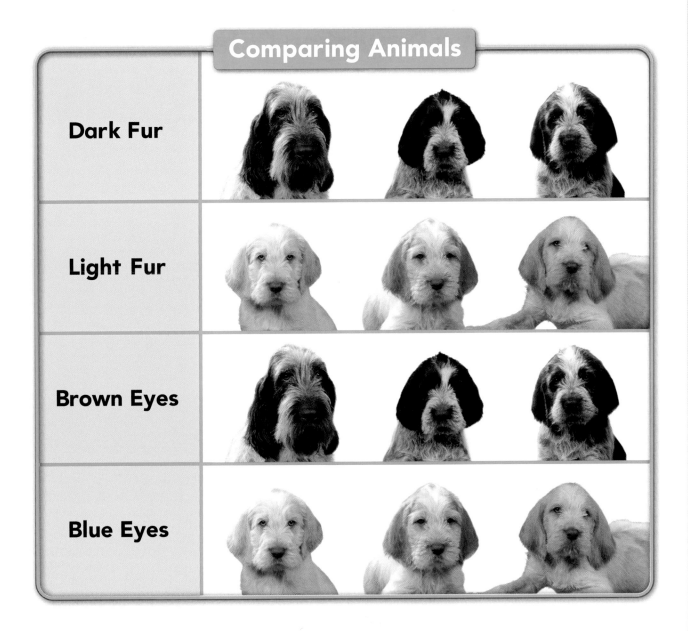

Dark Fur	
Light Fur	
Brown Eyes	
Blue Eyes	

An **individual** is one living thing in a group of the same kind of living things. The table shows how the traits of individuals in a family of dogs compare.

▶ **Main Idea** How do the animals in a family compare?

Activity Card 23
Compare Two Individuals

Animals in a Population Differ

Like animals in a family, animals in a population are not exactly alike. You learned that a population is a group of the same kind of living thing in one place.

Just like animals in a family, animals in a population are different because they inherit different traits. Their size may be different. Their height may be different. They may be a different color. Look at the horses shown below. Each one has different traits, but they all are horses.

a population of horses

Animals from the same parents may look different for another reason. The environment may affect the animals. An animal may not get the same amount of food as another. An animal may get too much food. If an animal gets sick, it may not grow to be as large as others in the population.

▶ **Main Idea** How can animals in the same population differ?

These individual horses look different, but they are part of the same population.

Lesson Wrap-Up

❶ **Vocabulary** What is an **individual**?

❷ **Reading Skill** List two ways that animals from one family may be alike.

❸ **Measure** How can measuring show differences in animals?

Technology Visit **www.eduplace.com/gascp** to find out more about animal differences.

STANDARDS S2CS2b. Readily give the sums and differences of single-digit numbers in ordinary, practical contexts and judge the reasonableness of the answer. **M2N2a.** Correctly add and subtract two whole numbers up to three digits each with regrouping. **ELA2W1a.** Writes text of length appropriate to address a topic and tell a story.

Math Add the Animals

Kim and Aisha saw many animals at Zoo Atlanta. They saw 2 pandas, 2 tigers, 3 elephants, 23 gorillas, and 1 leopard. How many animals did they see in all?

 **Describe a Life Cycle**

Think about what happens in each stage of a frog's life cycle. Write an adventure story about a frog's life. Tell it from the frog's point of view. Make a drawing to go with your story.

Performance Task

How do animals change as they grow?

Describe each stage of an animal's life cycle.

• Use a different card to draw each stage of an animal's life cycle.

• On the back of each card write how the animal changes.

• Mix up your cards. Then trade cards with another group.

• Order the other group's cards.

• How did the animals change as they grew?

STANDARDS S2CS6d. All different kinds of people can be and are scientists.

Animal Nutritionist

Nutrition is another word for food. An animal nutritionist is a person who chooses healthy food for animals.

Some animal nutritionists help farmers and ranchers feed their animals. Others work at zoos or aquariums. Their job is to keep animals well fed and healthy.

What It Takes!

- At least four years of college
- An interest in animals and science

People in Science

 STANDARDS S2CS6d. All different kinds of people can be and are scientists.

Dr. Ray Wack

Meet Dr. Ray Wack. He is a veterinarian, or a doctor who takes care of animals. He works at a zoo. He cares for many kinds of animals.

Zoo animals are not pets. They come from wild places around the world. Dr. Wack hopes that everyone will protect the wild places where animals live.

This baby animal was born at a zoo. A veterinarian helps take care of it.

Visual Summary

Animals are much like other animals of the same kind. But in some ways they are different.

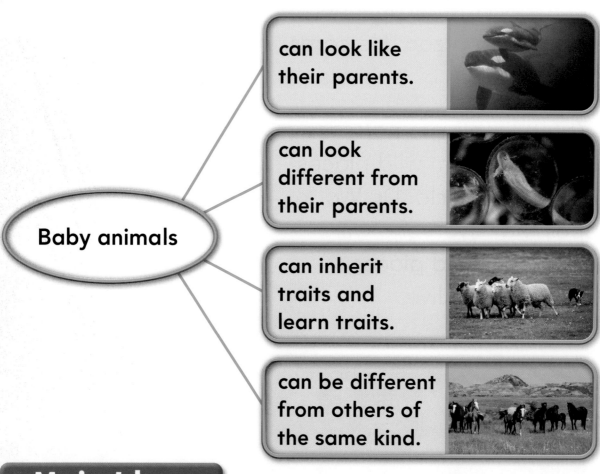

Baby animals

can look like their parents.

can look different from their parents.

can inherit traits and learn traits.

can be different from others of the same kind.

Main Ideas

1. How are the life cycles of a bird and a mouse alike and different? **(pp. 250–251)** `S2L1a`

2. Where do animals get their inherited traits? **(pp. 262–263)** `S2L1a`

3. How can animals of the same kind be different? **(pp. 270–271)** `S2L1a`

Vocabulary

Choose the correct word from the box.

4. One living thing in a group of the same kind of living things

5. The living things that come from a living thing

6. To make more living things of the same kind

7. The stage when an insect changes form

S2CS7a

reproduce (p. 248)

offspring (p. 248)

pupa (p. 256)

individual (p. 271)

Using Science Skills

8. You find a larva on a leaf. How do you think it will change over time? **S2L1a**

9. **Critical Thinking** What is a trait that you inherited? What is a trait that you learned? **S2L1a**

GPS CRCT Prep

Choose the best answer.

10. Which statement below is true?

(A) Mice are born from eggs.

(B) A tadpole's tail disappears as it grows.

(C) A pupa does not become a butterfly. **S2L1a**

GPS Test Practice

Choose the correct answer.

1. In which plant part do seeds form?

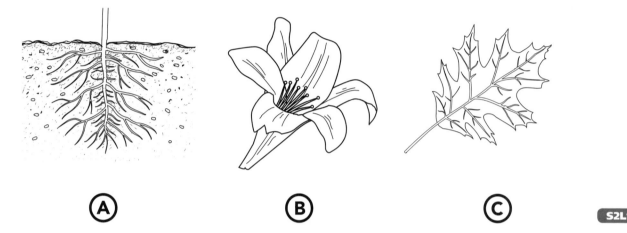

Ⓐ   Ⓑ   Ⓒ   S2L1c

2. What might cause one plant to grow tall and another to die?

gravity   fruit   environment

Ⓐ   Ⓑ   Ⓒ   S2L1c

3. What is the stage that comes next after this stage?

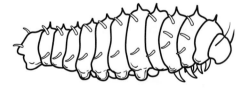

egg   adult   pupa

Ⓐ   Ⓑ   Ⓒ   S2L1a

4. What do baby birds look most like?

eggs   baby mice   their parents

Ⓐ   Ⓑ   Ⓒ   S2L1a

5. What will these seeds grow into?

tomato plant   a pine tree   a pea plant

Ⓐ   Ⓑ   Ⓒ   S2L1c

GPS Checking Main Ideas

Write the correct answer.

6. Choose a plant or animal. Write about its life cycle.

                                            S2L1a

                                            S2L1c

7. How are seeds important to plants?

You Can...

 STANDARDS S2CS4d. Compare very different sizes, weights, ages (baby/adult), and speeds (fast/slow) of both human made and natural things.

Discover More

How do mother sea lions find their pups?

To find their pups, mother sea lions make a loud trumpet sound. Each mother's sound is different. When the pup hears the sound, it makes a bleating sound back. Mother and pup continue until they find each other. The mother knows for sure which pup is hers by its smell.

 Go to **www.eduplace.com/gascp** to learn how animals find their babies.

Science and Math Toolbox

Using a Hand Lens H2

Using a Thermometer H3

Using a Ruler H4

Using a Calculator H5

Using a Balance H6

Making a Chart H7

Making a Tally Chart H8

Making a Bar Graph H9

Using a Hand Lens

A hand lens is a tool that makes objects look bigger. It helps you see the small parts of an object.

Look at a Coin

1 Place a coin on your desk.

STEP 1

2 Hold the hand lens above the coin. Look through the lens. Slowly move the lens away from the coin. What do you see?

3 Keep moving the lens away until the coin looks blurry.

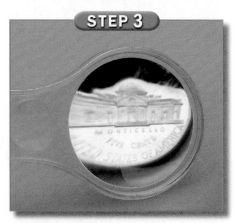

STEP 3

4 Then slowly move the lens closer. Stop when the coin does not look blurry.

STEP 4

Using a Thermometer

A thermometer is a tool used to measure temperature. Temperature tells how hot or cold something is. It is measured in degrees.

Find the Temperature of Water

1 Put water into a cup.

2 Put a thermometer into the cup.

3 Watch the colored liquid in the thermometer. What do you see?

4 Find the top of the red liquid. What number is next to it? That is the temperature of the water.

Using a Ruler

A ruler is a tool used to measure the length of objects. Rulers measure length in inches or centimeters.

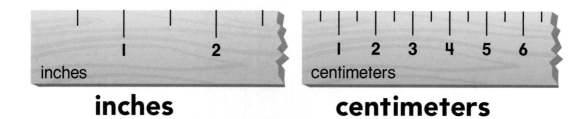

inches   **centimeters**

Measure a Crayon

1 Place the ruler on your desk.

2 Lay your crayon next to the ruler. Line up one end with the end of the ruler.

3 Look at the other end of the crayon. Which number is closest to that end?

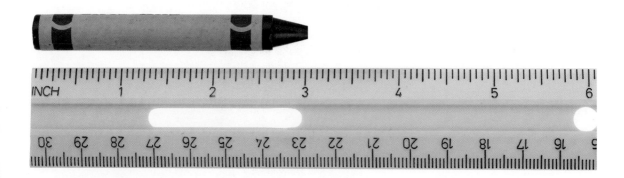

Using a Calculator

A calculator is a tool that can help you add and subtract numbers.

Subtract Numbers

1 Tim and Anna grew plants. Tim grew 5 plants. Anna grew 8 plants.

2 How many more plants did Anna grow? Use your calculator to find out.

3 Enter 8 on the calculator. Then press the – key. Enter 5 and press = .

What is your answer?

Tim's Plants

Anna's Plants

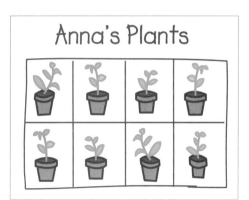

Using a Balance

A balance is a tool used to measure mass. Mass is the amount of matter in an object.

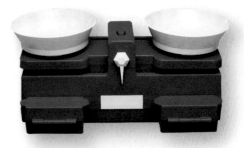

Compare the Mass of Objects

1. Check that the pointer is on the middle mark of the balance. If needed, move the slider on the back to the left or right.

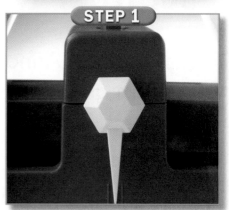

2. Place a clay ball in one pan. Place a crayon in the other pan.

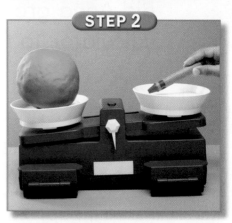

3. Observe the positions of the two pans.

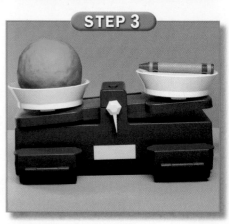

Does the clay ball or the crayon have more mass?

Making a Chart

A chart can help you sort information, or data. When you sort data it is easier to read and compare.

Make a Chart to Compare Animals

1 Give the chart a title.

2 Name the groups that tell about the data you collect. Label the columns with the names.

3 Carefully fill in the data in each column.

Which animal can move in the most ways?

How Animals Move

Animal	How It Moves
fish	swim
dog	walk, swim
duck	walk, fly, swim

Making a Tally Chart

A tally chart helps you keep track of items as you count.

Make a Tally Chart of Kinds of Pets

Jan's class made a tally chart to record the number of each kind of pet they own.

1 Every time they counted one pet, they made one tally.

2 When they got to five, they made the fifth tally a line across the other four.

3 Count the tallies to find each total.

How many of each kind of pet do the children have?

Kinds of Pets

🐱	cat	ЖЖ II
🐶	dog	ЖЖ III
🐹	hamster	III

Making a Bar Graph

A bar graph can help you sort and compare data.

Make a Bar Graph of Favorite Pets

You can use the data in the tally chart on page H8 to make a bar graph.

1 Choose a title for your graph.

2 Write numbers along the side.

3 Write pet names along the bottom.

4 Start at the bottom of each column. Fill in one box for each tally.

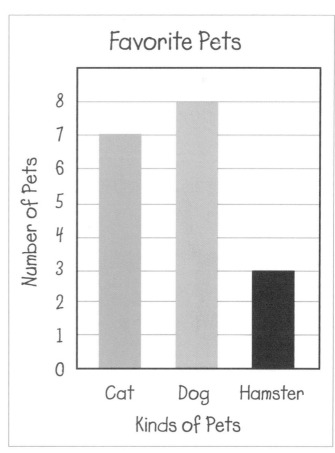

Which pet is the favorite?

Health and Fitness Handbook

When your body works well, you are healthy. Here are some ways to stay healthy.

- Know how your body works.

- Follow safety rules.

- Dance, jump, run, or swim to make your body stronger.

- Eat foods that give your body what it needs.

Your Senses.............................H12
Your senses tell you about the world around you.

Protect Eyes and Ears.....................H14
Learn how to protect your eyes and ears.

Staying Safe on the Road...............H15
Be safe when you walk or when you ride in a car or bus.

Move Your Muscles!..........................H16
There are many ways to exercise your muscles.

Food Groups.....................................H17
Eat foods from different groups.

Your Senses

Your five senses help you learn about the world. They help you stay safe.

Sight

Light enters the eye through the pupil. The iris controls how much light comes in. Other parts of the eye turn the light into messages that go to the brain.

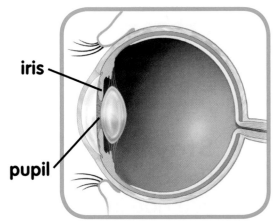

iris

pupil

The iris is the colored part of the eye.

Hearing

The ear has three main parts. Most of your ear is inside your head. Sound makes some parts of the ear move back and forth very fast. The inner ear sends information about the sound to the brain.

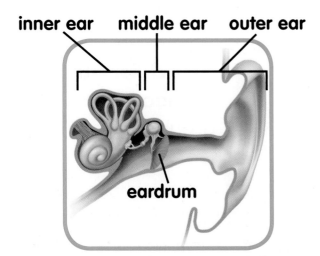

inner ear   middle ear   outer ear

eardrum

The eardrum is easily injured. Never stick anything in your ear.

Taste

Your tongue is covered with thousands of tiny bumps called taste buds. They help you taste sweet, salty, sour, and bitter things. Some parts of the tongue seem to sense some flavors more strongly. The whole tongue tastes salty foods.

Your body makes a new set of taste buds about every two weeks.

Smell

All kinds of smells travel through the air. These smells enter your nose. Your nose sends messages to your brain about them.

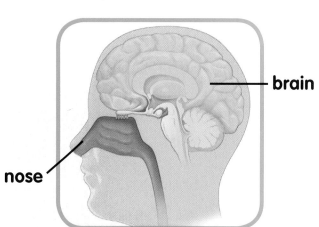

Your sense of smell also helps you taste.

Touch

Touch a tree trunk, and it feels rough. A kitten feels soft. Your skin senses all this information. Then the brain decides how to respond.

Your skin is your body's largest organ.

Protect Eyes and Ears

You use your eyes and ears to see and hear. You can protect your eyes and ears.

Protect Your Eyes

- Keep sharp things away from your eyes.

- Wear sunglasses when you are outside. They protect your eyes from the Sun's rays.

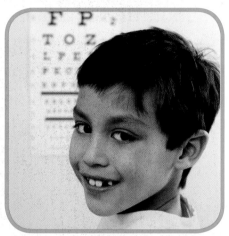

An eye test can help tell if a person needs glasses.

Protect Your Ears

- Wear a helmet when you play baseball or softball.

- Loud noises can damage your ears. Keep music at a low volume.

A hearing test tells if a person has a hearing loss.

Staying Safe on the Road

How do you get to school or a playground? Here are ways to help you stay safe.

Walk Safely

- Stay on the sidewalk.

- Walk with a friend or trusted adult.

- Cross at crosswalks. Look both ways before you cross!

- Don't run between parked cars. Drivers might not see you.

Only cross when the "walk" sign is lit.

Car and Bus Safety

- If a bus has seat belts, wear one.

- Stay seated and talk quietly so the driver can pay attention to the road.

- Cross the street in front of a bus after all traffic stops.

Obey crossing guards.

Always wear your seat belt in a car.

Move Your Muscles!

All kinds of things can be exercise. Here are some ways you can make your muscles stronger.

By Yourself

- Kick a ball as far as you can. Chase it and kick it back.

- Ride your bike.

- Jump rope.

- Do jumping jacks.

- Put on music and dance.

With Others

- Play ball!

- Play tag. Run!

- Go for a hike.

- Play hopscotch.

- Play with a flying disk.

Food Groups

Food gives your body energy and what your body needs to grow. Foods in different groups help you in different ways.

Milk

Meat and Beans

Fruits

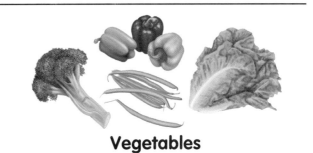

Vegetables

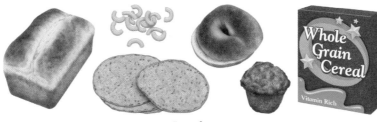

Grains

Pizza includes the Milk group (cheese), the Grains group (crust), and the Vegetable group (tomatoes).

What groups are in this bowl of cereal?

Picture Glossary

A

adult
An animal that is full grown. (249)

ask questions
Learn more about what you observe by asking questions of yourself and others.

C

classify
Sort objects into groups that are alike in some way.

communicate
Share what you learn with others by talking, drawing pictures, or making charts and graphs.

compare
Look for ways that objects or events are alike or different.

condenses
Changes from water vapor to drops of water. (19)

cone
Part of a nonflowering plant where seeds form. (212)

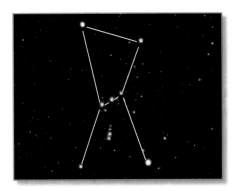

constellation
A group of stars that forms a picture. (78)

dissolves
Mixes completely with water. (115)

E

environment
All of the living and nonliving things around a living thing. (225)

evaporates
Changes to a gas. The Sun warms water, and water evaporates. (18)

Testing Magnets	
Position of the Magnets	What Happened

experiment
Make a plan to collect data and then share the results with others.

F

flower
The plant part where fruit and seeds form. (208)

force
A push or a pull. (146)

friction

A force that makes an object slow down when it rubs against another object. (148)

fruit

The part of a flower that grows around a seed. (208)

G

gas

A state of matter that spreads out to fill a space. A gas fills the inside of a balloon. (107)

gravity

Is a force that pulls all objects toward each other. (141, 232)

H

heat
A kind of energy that makes things warm. (172)

hibernate
To go into a deep sleep. (37)

I

individual
One living thing in a group of the same kind of living things. (271)

infer
Use what you observe and know to tell what you think.

inherit
To have traits passed on from the parent. (218)

L

larva
A worm-like stage in an insect's life cycle. (256)

learned
Traits that are not passed on from parents to their offspring. (264)

lever
A bar that moves around a fixed point. (159)

life cycle
The series of changes that a living thing goes through as it grows. (210)

light
A kind of energy that you can see. (180)

liquid
A state of matter that does not have its own shape. (106)

M

magnify

To make objects look larger. (124)

mass

The amount of matter in an object. You can measure mass with a balance. (109)

measure

Use different tools to collect data about the properties of objects.

melt

When heat is added a solid changes to a liquid. (175)

migrate

To move to warmer places in fall. (37)

mixture

Something made of two or more things. (114)

Moon

A large sphere made of rock. (68)

motion

Moving from one place to another. (140)

O

observe

Use tools and the senses to learn about the properties of an object or event.

offspring

The group of living things that come from the same living thing. (248)

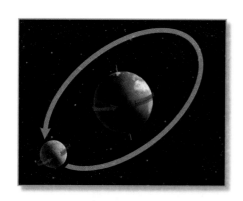

orbit
The path that one space object travels around another. (60)

phases
The different ways the moon looks. (70)

planet
A large object that moves around the Sun. (52)

population
A group of the same kind of living thing in one place. (226)

position
A place or location. The bird is on top of the cactus. (138)

precipitation
Water that falls from clouds. (20)

predict
Use what you know and patterns you observe to tell what will happen.

properties
Color, shape, size, odor, and texture. A penny is small and round. (104)

pulley
A wheel with a groove through which a rope or chain moves. (160)

pupa
The stage between larva and adult when an insect changes form. (256)

R

ramp
A slanted tool used to move things from one level to another. (158)

record data
Write or draw to show what you have observed.

reproduce
To make more living things of the same kind. (248)

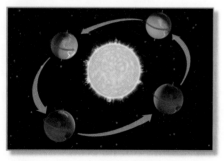

revolve
To move in a path around an object. (60)

rotates
Spins around an imaginary line. (58)

S

season
A time of year. (26)

seed
The part from which a new plant grows. (208)

separate
To take apart. (114)

simple machine
A tool that can make it easier to move objects. (158)

solar system

The Sun and the space objects that move around it. (52)

solid

A state of matter that has its own size and shape. (106)

star

A big ball of hot gases that gives off light. (76)

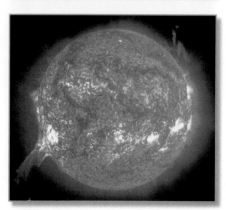

Sun

The brightest object in the day sky. (50)

use data

Use what you observe and record to find patterns and make predictions.

use models
Use something like the real thing to understand how the real thing works.

Length of Triops	
Day 1	about _____ cm
Day 2	about _____ cm
Day 3	about _____ cm
Day 4	about _____ cm
Day 5	about _____ cm

use numbers
Count, measure, order, or estimate to describe and compare objects and events.

volume
The amount of space a liquid takes up. (108)

water cycle
Water moving from Earth to the air and back again. (18)

water vapor

Water as a gas. You cannot see water vapor. (18)

work together

Work as a group to share ideas, data, and observations.

Acorns, 220–221
Adelgids, wooly, 6
Air temperature
   measuring, 15, 26–27,
      49, 231
Amphibians, 254–255
Anglerfish, 184
Animals
   alpacas, 266–267
   baby animals, 246–249,
      252–253
   changes caused by, 6–7
   changes in, 36–37
   color of, 36
   differences in, 268–273
   fur of, 36
   hibernation of, 37
   life cycle of, 193,
      242–245, 250–251
   migration of, 37
   population and,
      272–273
   seasons and, 36–37
   traits of, 244, 260–265,
      270–273
   vocabulary on, 248,
      262, 270
Animator, 161
Astronaut, 81
Axis, 58

Balance, 102, 159, H6
Big Dipper, 78
Birds, 250–251
Botanist, 238
Builder, 127
Butterflies, 37, 256–257

Caldeiro, Fernando,
   S2–S3
Cats, 262
Charts, 40, 67, 82, 162,
   171, 217, 231
**Chattahoochee National
   Forest,** 4–5
Chihuly, Dale, 111
Clouds, 18–19
Condensation, 19
Cones, 198–199, 212–213
Constellations, 54–55,
   74–75, 79–80
Crickets, S6–S7
Cryobot, S11

Day and night, 28–29,
   76–77
Daylight hours, 28–29,
   41
Decision-making,
   S14–S15
Deer, 36
Directed Inquiry, 15, 25,
   33, 49, 57, 67, 75, 103,
   113, 123, 137, 145, 155,
   171, 179, 207, 217, 223,
   231, 247, 253, 261, 269
Direction, changing, 149
Dissolve, 115
Dogs, 270–271

Ears, H14
Earth
   movement of, 56–61
   orbit of, 60–61

   revolution of, 60–61
   rotation of, 58–61
   solar system and, 52–53
   stars and, 77
Eggs
   of birds, 250–251
   of frogs, 254–255
   of insects, 256
Environment
   changes to, 5–7
   examples of, 225–227,
      230–235
Evaporation, 18
Exercise, H16
Eyes, H14

Fall, 26, 29, 34–35
Fire, 5
Fireflies, 184
Fish, 260–261
Flooding, 17
Flowers, 208–209, 211,
   218–219, 226
Food groups, H17
Forces, 144–148
Forests, 4–5
French, Lloyd, S10
Friction, 148
Frogs, 254–255
Fruits, 208–209, 211
Fungi, 214–215

Galerina mushrooms,
   215
Gases, 106–107

Georgia
  insects in, 6–7
  places in, 4–7, 166–167, 172
trees in, 4–7, 198–199
Glass, 110–111
Goldfish, 260–261
Grapes, 228–229
Graphs
  bar, 223, 268, H9
Gravity, 141, 232

Hail, 19–21
Hand lens, 123, 124–125, 207, 253, H2
Hands-On Projects, 8–9, 96–97, 200–201
Handspans, 269
Health and Fitness, H10–H17
Heat
  energy from, 174–175
  sources of, 166–167, 170–173, 176–177
  from Sun, 18, 28, 48–51
  using, 174–175
  vocabulary on, 172
Height, 217
Hibernation, 13, 37
Horses, 272–273

Individual, 271, 273
Inherited traits, 218–219, 224, 260, 262–263, 270–273
Inquiry Process, S8–S9

Inquiry Skills
  ask questions, 25, 136–137, 217, 247, 253
  be inventor, 33, 123
  classify, 246–247
  communicate, 24–25, 123, 207
  compare, 32–33, 74–75, 103, 112–113, 123, 144–145, 171, 179, 207, 216–217, 231, 247, 269
  experiment, 15, 49, 75, 113, 155, 171, 178–179, 207, 223, 231, 261, 269
  infer, 15, 25, 33, 49, 57, 113, 155, 171, 179, 207, 217, 253, 261
  measure, 15, 25, 102–103, 145, 154–155, 170–171, 217, 223, 231, 253, 268–269
  observe, 15, 56–57, 67, 122–123, 137, 145, 179, 206–207, 217, 247, 253
  predict, 48–49, 113, 145, 171, 223, 231, 260–261
  record data, 25, 49, 67, 137, 171, 223, 230–231, 247, 261, 269
  use data, 155, 252–253
  use models, 66–67, 75
  use numbers, 14–15, 222–223, 269
  work together, 57, 67, 103, 145
Insects, 6–7, 184, 244, 256–257
Inventor, S10–S13
Investigations, *See* Directed Inquiry

Ladybird beetles, 7
Lakes, 19
Larva, 256
Learned traits, 260–261, 264–265
Leaves, 34–35, 196–197
Length, 145, 155, 162, 223, 253, 269
Levers, 159
Life cycles
  of amphibians, 254–255
  of animals, 193, 242–245, 250–251, 262–265, 270–273
  comparing, 246–247
  of insects, 244, 256–257
  of plants, 193, 202, 206, 210–213, 218–221, 224–227
  of trees, 196-199, 212–213
  vocabulary on, 248, 254
Light
  energy from, 178–181
  sources of, 166–167
  from Sun, 48–51, 76
  using, 182–183
  vocabulary on, 180–181
Lightning, 5, 16–17, 22-23
Liquids, 106–108
Litter, S14–S15
Little Dipper, 78
Lizards, S4–S5
Longleaf pine tree, 198–199

Magnifying tools, 123, 124–126, 207, 253, H2
Mammals, 250–251

Index

Mass
  measuring, 103
  vocabulary on, 109
Math Link, 40, 82, 128,
  162, 186, 236, 274
Matter
  changes in, 116–121
  comparing, 98–101
  observing, 122–126
  states of, 106–107
  vocabulary on, 114
Measuring
  height, 217
  length, 145, 155, 162,
    223, 253
  mass, 103
  temperature, 15, 25, 33,
    49, 171
  volume, 103
Melting, 175
Meteorologists, 17, 39
Microscope, 124–125
Migration, 12, 37
Mixtures, 114–115
Monarch butterflies, 37
Monkeys, 265
Moon
  composition of, 68, 72
  charts of, 70–71, 82
  craters on, 68
  legends of, 72
  movement of, 66–70
  phases of, 66–67, 70–71
  reflecting sunlight, 70
  revolution of, 69
  rocks on, 68
  solar system and, 52–53
  Sun and, 70, 73
  vocabulary on, 68
Motion
  direction and, 149
  forces and, 144–148
  friction and, 148
  measuring, 154–157
  observing, 132–133,
    136–137
  position and, 134, 138,
    140–141

  safety and, 150-153
  speed and, 92–95
  using, 146–147
  vocabulary on, 146, 156
Mouse, 250–251
Muscles, H16
Mushrooms, 214–215

NASA, 81
Night and day, 28–29,
  76–77
North Star, 78

Oak trees, 220–221
Objects
  describing, 104–105
  measuring, 108–109
  observing, 122–126
  position of, 138,
    140–141
  properties of, 104–105
  vocabulary on, 104, 138
Ocean animals, S14–S15
Oceans, 19
Ochoa, Dr. Ellen, 81
Offspring, 248–249
Orbit, 60–61
Orion, 54–55, 79

Pea plant, 208
Pea pods, 223
Penguins, 249
Performance Tasks, 7,
  41, 83, 95, 129, 163,
  187, 199, 237, 275

Pine tree, 198–199,
  212–213
Planets, 52–53. *See also*
  Solar system
Plants
  changes caused by, 5
  changes in, 34–35
  differences in, 222–227
  environment and, 205,
    225–227, 230–235
  flowers and, 204,
    208–209, 211,
    218–219, 226
  fruits and, 208–209, 211
  gravity and, 232
  growth of, 211
  life cycle of, 193, 202,
    206, 210–213
  parent plants, 211,
    218–219, 221
  parts of, 208
  seasons and, 34–35
  seeds and, 203, 208,
    210–213, 216–218,
    230–231
  soil and, 7
  traits of, 218–219, 224
  vocabulary on, 203,
    208, 224, 232
Polaris, 78
Population, 226–227,
  272–273
Position, 138
Precipitation, 13, 19–21
Properties, 104–105
Pueblo Indians, 176–177
Puffballs, 214
Pulleys, 160
Pupa, 256–257

Rabbits, 248
Radar, 17
Rain, 17, 19–21

Ramps, 158
Reading Skills
    categorize and classify,
      104, 107, 109
    cause and effect, 146,
      180, 232,
    compare and
      contrast, 34, 76, 156,
      224, 248
    draw conclusions,
      58, 61, 114, 138,
      218, 262
    main idea and
      details, 16, 50, 124,
      172, 270
    sequence, 26, 208, 254
Reproduce, 248
Revolutions, 60–61, 69
Rivers, 19
Robots, S10–S11
Roots, 232
Rotation, 58–61

Safety tips, S16, 3031,
    150–153, H15
Science Inquiry, S6–S7
Scientists, S2–S8
Seasons
    animals and, 36–37
    changes in, 32–38
    clothing for, 38
    daylight and, 28
    Earth's orbit and, 61
    leaves and, 196–197
    pattern of, 24–29, 61
    plants and, 34–35
    trees and, 196–197
    vocabulary on, 34
Seedlings, 212–213
Seeds
    fruits and, 208–209, 211

plants and, 203, 208,
    210–213, 216–218,
    230–231
    sprouting, 230–231
Senses, H12–H13
Separate, 114–115
Shadows, 57, 59, 62–65
Sheep, 264
Simple machines,
    158–160
Silver maple tree,
    196–197
Skunks, 264
Sleet, 19–21
Snow, 19–21
Snowdrifts, 21
Snowstorms, 21
Soil, 7, 232
Solar system
    planets and, 50–53
    stars and, 44–45
    Sun and, 47–53
    vocabulary on, 50
Solids, 106–108
Speed, 92–95, 142–143,
    192
Spores, 214–215
Spring, 26, 34–35
Squirrels, 37
Stars
    brightness, 50,
      76–77
    constellations and,
      74–75, 78–80
    differences in, 76–77
    Earth and, 77
    patterns of, 54–55,
      78–79
    size of, 54–55, 76–77
    solar system and,
      44–45
    vocabulary on, 76
Storms, 17, 20
Streams, 19
Summer, 26, 28–29,
    34–35, 61

Sun
    energy from, 50–51
    heat from, 18, 28,
      48–51
    light from, 48–51, 76
    Moon and, 70, 73
    rays of, 30–31
    safety in, 30–31
    size of, 50
    solar system and,
      47–53
Sundial, 57
Sunlight, 30, 70, 233

Tadpoles, 254–255
Technology, S11
Temperatures, 26–27,
    171
Thermometers, 15, 25,
    33, 49, 171, 231, H3
Thunderstorms, 17, 20
Tomato plant, 210–211
Tools
    balance, 102, 159, H6
    bar graphs, 223, 268,
      H9
    calculators, H5
    charts, H7–H8
    hand lens, 123, 207,
      253, H2
    rulers, 145, 155, 162,
      223, 253, 269, H4
    thermometers, 15, 25,
      33, 49, 171,
      231, H3
Tortoises, 248
Traits
    of animals, 244,
      260–265, 270–273
    inherited traits,
      218–219, 224, 260,
      262–263, 270–273

Index

learned traits,
244, 260–261,
264–265
of plants, 218–219, 224
Trees
acorns and, 220–221
changes in, 34–35,
196–197
in Georgia, 4–7,
196–199
gravity and, 232
life cycle of, 212–213
seasons and, 196–197
seeds from, 220–221
Triops eggs, 252–253
Troutman, Tracey, 239

Use Numbers, 14–15

Volume, 108

Wack, Dr. Ray, 277
Water, 18–19

Water cycle, 18–19
Water vapor, 18–19
Weather
changes caused by, 5,
17, 21
changes in, 14–17, 38
patterns of, 10–11, 16,
26–27
study of, 39
vocabulary on, 16, 26
Weather radar, 17
Whales, 249
Wind, 20–21
Winter, 26, 34–35, 61
Wooly adelgids
effects of, 6–7
Writing Link, 40, 82, 128,
162, 186, 234, 236, 274

Credits

Permission Acknowledgements

Storm from *Swing Around the Sun* by Barbara Juster Esbensen, illustrated by Janice Lee Porter. Text copyright © 1965 by Lerner Publications Company, © 2003 by Carolrhoda Books, Inc. Summer artwork copyright © 2003 by Janice Lee Porter. Reprinted by permission of Carolrhoda Books, Inc., a division of Lerner Publishing Group, Inc. All rights reserved. No part of this excerpt may be used or reproduced in any manner whatsoever without the prior written permission of Lerner Publishing Group, Inc. From *The Tale of Rabbit and Coyote* by Tony Johnston, copyright © 1998 by Roger D. Johnston and Susan T. Johnston as Trustees of the Johnston Family Trust. Used by permission of G.P. Putnam's Sons, A Division of Penguin Young Readers Group, A Member of Penguin Group (USA) Inc., 345 Hudson Street, New York, NY 10014. All rights reserved. *The Starry Sky: The Sun and Moon* by Patrick Moore, illustrated by Paul Doherty. Copyright © 1994 by Aladdin Books Limited. Text copyright © 1994 by Patrick Moore. Revised edition © 2000. Reprinted by permission of Aladdin Children's Books. *The Steam Shovel* by Rowena Bennett. Copyright © 1948 by Rowena Bennett. Reprinted by permission of Kenneth Bennett. *Caterpillar* by Mary Dawson. Copyright © Mary Dawson. Our best efforts have been made to locate the rights holder of this selection. If anyone has any information as to the whereabouts of the author or her representatives, please contact the School Permissions Department, Houghton Mifflin Company, 222 Berkeley Street, Boston, MA 02116.

Cover and Title Page

Front cover (Garibaldi) © Gregory Ochocki/ Photo Researchers, Inc. (water background) © Flip Nicklin/Minden Pictures. Back cover © Flip Nicklin/Minden Pictures. Spine © Gregory Ochocki/Photo Researchers, Inc. Title page © Gregory Ochocki/Photo Researchers, Inc. End Paper (t) Brandon D. Cole/Corbis. (b) © 1994 M.C. Chamberlain/ DRK Photo.

Photography

iv–v ©James Randklev. vi ©Michael Holahan/The Augusta Cronicle. viii © Joseph G. Strauch, Jr. ix ©Dutcher, Jim & Jamie/ngsimages. Sii ©Scott L. Robertson S1 ©Skip Moody/Dembinsky Photo Associates, Inc. S2 Courtesy of Six Flags Over Georgia. S6 ©Wesley Hitt/Mira.com. UAUO Terrance Klassen/Alamy Images. 2–3 ©Gene & Karen Rhoden/Bruce Coleman, Inc. 4–5 (bkgrd) ©James Randklev. (t) Visions of America, LLC/Joe Sohm/Alamy Images. (b) Rex Stucky/ National Geogr-aphic/Getty Images. 6–7 (bkgrd) ©Michael Godomski/Animals Animals. (c) ©Alan & Linda Detrick/Science Photo Library/Photo Researchers, Inc. (b) ©Ted Kinsman/Photo Researchers, Inc. (inset) ©Connie Toops. 8 Derrick Alderman/ Alamy Images. 10–11 (bkgrd) ©Warren Faidley/Weather Stock. 11 (t) Oswald Eckstein/zefa/Corbis. (cl) John Anderson/ Alamy Images. (t) ©Michael Mahovlich/ Masterfile. 12 ©Jacana/Photo Researchers, Inc. 13 (t) ©Andy Crawford/DK. (cl) ©Gary Meszaros/Photo Researchers, Inc. (b) Jeff Foott/Jupiter Images. 14–15 (bkgrd) Royalty-Free/Corbis. (b) ©Frank LaBua/ Photri-Microstock. 16–17 (b)©Don Nauman. (inset) ©NOAA NATIONAL HURRICAN CENTER/APIMAGES. 18–19 (bkgrd)©Jim Steinberg/Photo Researchers, Inc. 20 (cl) ©Gary Meszaros/Photo Researchers, Inc. (b) ©Scott Smith/Index Stock. 21 ©Jim Mone/Associated Press. 24–25 (bkgrd) ©Caroll Mallory/Dembinsky Photo Associates, Inc. (b) ©Kike Calvo/Bruce Coleman, Inc. 26 ©Dawn Charging. 27 ©Michael Holahan/The Augusta Cronicle. 32–33 (bkgrd) ©Maslowski Photo/Photo Researchers, Inc. (bl) ©Sid & Shirley Rucker/DRK Photo. 34 (cl) ©Bill Beatty. (br) ©Michael Gadomski/Photo Research-ers, Inc. 35 (tl) ©Harry Rogers/Photo Researchers, Inc. (bl) © blickwinkel/Alamy (tc) ©Thase Daniel/Bruce Coleman, Inc. (bc) © Iconotec/Alamy. (tr) ©Edward I. Snow/Bruce Coleman, Inc. (br) © Janice Hazeldine/Alamy. 36–37 (b) ©Fred Bruemmer/DRK Photo. (bl) ©Fred Habegger/Photri-Microstock. (br) ©Daniel J Cox/Natural Selection Stock. (tr) ©Jeff Foott/Jupiter Images. (c) S. Charles Brown; Frank Lane Picture Agency/Corbis. (inset) ©Bill Beatty/Animals Animals. 39 (b) Joe Daedele/Getty Images. (bkgrd) ©Tom Pantages Stock Photos. 42 (l) ©Edward l. Snow/Bruce Coleman, Inc. (c) ©Bill Beatty. (cr) ©Harry Rogers/Photo Researchers, Inc. (r) ©Thase Daniel/Bruce Coleman, Inc. (bl) ©Jeff Foott/Jupiter Images. (bc) S. Charles Brown; Frank Lane Picture Agency/Corbis. (br) ©Bill Beatty/Animals Animals. (r) ©Fred Bruemmer/DRK Photo. 44–45 (bkgrd) ©John Henry Williams/Bruce Coleman, Inc. (tr) ©Frank Zullo/Photo Researchers, inc. (cl)©Stock Connection Distribution/Alamy Images. (c) ©Royalty-Free/Corbis. (c) Corbis. 46–47 (bkgrd) ©John Sanford/ Photo Researchers, Inc. (cl) Roger Ressmeyer/Corbis. 48–49 (bkgrd) ©Nasa/ Photri-Microstock. (b) Nasa/Photri-Microstock. 50 (t) ©NASA/Science Photo Library/Photo Researchers, Inc. 51 (b) ©Klein/Hubert/Peter Arnold, Inc. 56–57 (bkgrd) ©Bill Aron/Photo Edit, Inc. 56 (b) World Perspectives/Photographer's choice/ Getty Images. 59 ©Colin Young-Wolff/ Photo Edit, Inc. 66–67 (bkgrd) Steven Satushek/Botanica/ Getty Images. 66 (b) World Perspectives/ Stone/Getty Images. 68 (b) World Perspectives/Stone/Getty Images. 70–71 (bkgrd) ©John Sanford/Photo Researchers, Inc. 76–77 (bkgrd) Michael Simpson/Taxi/ Getty Images. (l) ©Eckhard Slawk/Photo Researchers, Inc. (r) Photri-Microstock. (l) ©Susan Mccartney/Photo Researchers, Inc. (r)Photri-Microstock. 78 (b) Roger Ressmeyer/Corbis. 79 (tl) Roger Ressmeyer/Corbis. (br) ©John Sanford & David Parker/Science Photo Library/Photo Researchers, Inc. 81 (bl) ©NASA/Photo Reserarchers, Inc. (br) Photri-Microstock. (bkgrd) StockTrek/Photodisc/Getty Images. 84 (r)©John Sanford/Photo Researchers, Inc. 88 (l) David Stoecklein/Corbis. (c) Randy Faris/Corbis. (r) Larry Gilpin/Stone/ Getty Images. UBUO (bkgrd) ©Jeff Greenberg/The Image Works. UB01–89 ©Baby Face/Jupiterimages. 92–93 ©Scott L. Robertson. 94 ©Courtesy of Six Flags Over Georgia. 98–99 (bkgrd) Everett Kennedy Brown, staff/European Press Photo Agency, EPA. (t) S.T. Yiap/Alamy Images. (cl) Corbis Premium Collection/ Alamy Images. (b) ©Michael Newman/ Photo Edit, Inc. 100 ©Susan Findlay/ Masterfile. 102–103 (bkgrd) Thom Lang/ Corbis. (cr) Thom Lang/Corbis. (c) Terrance Klassen/Alamy Images. (bl)©Gusto/Photo Researchers, Inc. 109 (br) G K & Vikki Hart/ Getty Images. 120 ©Hmco/APEX. 121 (bc) Image Courtesy of the United States Mint. (br,bl) ©Hmco/APEX. 122–123 (bkgrd) George D. Lepp/Corbis. (b) ©Skip Moody/ Dembinsky Photo Associates, Inc. 124 Ralph A. Clevenger/Corbis. 125 (t) Jose Luis Pelaez, Inc./Corbis. (tr) ©Iverson/Folio, Inc. (bl) Jim Zuckerman/Corbis. (br) ©Greg Wahl- Stephens/Associated Press. 126 (tl) ©Mark A. Schneider/Dembinsky Photo Associates. (tc) ©Skip Moody/Dembinsky Photo Associates. (tr) Darrell Gulin/Corbis. (bl) ©Iverson/Folio, Inc. (bc) ©Iverson/Folio, Inc. (br) Clouds Hill Imaging Ltd./Corbis. 127 (c) ©Steve Cole/Masterfile. 133 (tr) ©BananaStock/Agefotostock. 134–135 (bkrgd) ©Tony Freeman/Photo Edit, Inc. (c) BOB Daemmrich/Corbis. (b) ©Phil Degginger/ Color Pic, Inc. 136–137 Thinkstock/Getty Images. 140 (l) ©Tony Freeman/Photo Edit, Inc. (r) ©Picture Plain/Photo Library. 141 (t) John Fox/Alamy Images. (r) RubberBall Productions/Getty Images. 144–145 (bkgrd) Rolf Bruderer/Corbis. (b) Rolf Bruderer/Corbis. 147 (br) © Chuck Franklin/Alamy. 148 ©Philip Gatward/DK Images. 149 Rubberball Productions/Getty Images. 156–157 (b),David Madison/Stone/ Getty Images. (t) Alan Thornton/Stone/ Getty Images. 158 BOB Daemmrich/Corbis. 159 (t) ©E. R. Degginger/Color Pic, Inc. (c) ©Phil Degginger/Color Pic, Inc. 160 (l) ©Kimberly Robbins/Photo Edit, Inc. 161 ©Mark Spess. 162 Raymond K Gehman/ National Geographic/Getty Images. 164 (tc) © Chuck Franklin/Alamy. (tr) ©Philip Gatward/DK Images. (bl) John Fox/Alamy Images. (bc) ©Picture Plain/Photo Library. (br) ©Tony Freeman/Photo Edit, Inc. 166–167 (bkgrd) ©Raymond K Gehman/ National Geographic/Getty Images. (tr) Joy Stein/ShutterStock. (c) Photo Link/ Photodisc/Getty Images. 168–169 (bkgrd) ©Scott L. Robertson. (tc) ©Kevin Barry. 170 Photo Link/Photodisc/Getty Images. 172 ©Kevin Barry 173 (inset) ©Bill Aron/Photo Edit, Inc. 176–177 (bkgrd) ©Miles Ertman/Masterfile. (cl) ©Peter Anderson/DK Images. (cr) ©David R. Frazier/Photo Researchers, Inc. 178 ©Peter Batson/Image Quest Marine. 180 Grace/Zefa/Corbis. 181 (b) Dorling Kindersley/Getty Images. (t) 2000 Paul Cunningham/Getty Images. 182 (bkgrd) ©Scott L. Robertson. 183 (t) Kelly-Mooney Photography/Corbis. 188 (tl) Photolink/ Photodisc/Getty Images. (tc) ©Kevin Barry. (cl) ©Scott L. Robertson. (c) Dorling Kindersley/Getty Images. (cr) Kelly-Mooney/Corbis. 189 Baby Face/ Jupiter Images. UCUO ©David Welling/ Animals Animals. UC01–193 ©Dutcher, Jim & Jamie/ngsimages. 194–195 (bkgrd) ©Charles Mann/Photo Researchers, Inc. 196–197 (bkgrd) ©Ed Jackson. (b) ©David Cavagnaro/DRK photo. (c) Martin B. Withers; Frank Lane Picture Agency/Corbis. (t) © Rod Planck/Photo Researchers, Inc. 198 (bkgrd) ©Graeme Teague Photography. (cl) ©Patti Murray/Photolibrary. (cr)

Assignment

Illustration

Extreme Science

Nature of Science

Health and Fitness Handbook

Science and Math Toolbox

Picture Glossary